RAIL CENTRES:
SWINDON

RAIL CENTRES:
SWINDON

COLIN G. MAGGS

Nottingham

Booklaw Publications

First published 1983 by Ian Allan Ltd

©C. G. Maggs 1983

This edition published 2007 by Booklaw Publications
382, Carlton Hill, Nottingham NG4 1JA

ISBN 1-901945-13-8

Printed by
The Amadeus Press, Cleckheaton, West Yorkshire

Acknowledgements
Grateful acknowledgement for assistance is due to:
L. Barrett (Pressed Steel Fisher Ltd); R. Biggs, S. Bolan,
P. Brown (Area Manager, BR, Swindon), J. M.
Cummings, M. E. J. Deane, D. Durbridge (Pressed Steel
Fisher Ltd), C. R. C. Eddolls (Coopers [Metals]
Ltd), R. de Graff (Divisional Librarian, Swindon), E. G.
Jefferies (BREL), Miss M. Hole, D. J. Hyde, Miss
M. Newman, J. R. Robson and D. R. Steggles. I. Huddy
has special thanks for checking the manuscript.

Contents

Front cover, top: 'King' class No 6018 *King Henry VI*
seen at Swindon with an SLS Special on 28 April 1963.
Hugh Ballantyne

Front cover, bottom: Class 253 unit No 253.015 passes
Swindon with the 08.15 Paddington-Bristol in January
1977. *T. G. Flinders*

Front endpaper: Swindon scrapyard 1892 style. Broad
gauge engines awaiting conversion or scrapping.
Real Photos

Rear endpaper: Class 253 unit, No 253 001
approaching Swindon on 24 June 1976 while on a
driver training run. *Brian Morrison*

Title page, right: Swindon Junction, view up 1909.
GWR

Title page, left: Brush Type 4, Class 47, No 1942 stands
at Swindon with 1B26, a Paddington-Bristol working.
7 March 1973. *N. E. Preedy*

Left: Class 47/0 No 47.011 passing Swindon on 24 June
1976 with down tanker train. *Brian Morrison*

Outline history

Old Swindon built on a hill rising to almost 500ft above sea level, has provided a home for man from Neolithic times. Mentioned in the Domesday Book, it developed into a principal market town, sufficiently important in later years to be situated on a canal, the Wilts & Berks arriving in June 1804 and linking the Thames at Abingdon with the Kennet & Avon near Melksham, while the North Wilts Canal opened on 2 April 1819 linking Swindon with the Thames & Severn Canal.

Plans for building a broad gauge rail link from London to Bristol, then the second largest city in the kingdom, were passed by Parliament on 31 August 1835, the Great Western Railway skirting the foot of the hill on which Swindon was built. As with modern motorways, the length was too great to be completed at once in its entirety and so was opened in stages; the length to Faringdon Road, (renamed Challow in 1864), 13 miles east of Swindon, opened on 20 July 1840. The wet winter delayed work on the section from Faringdon Road to Chippenham and the Great Western directors decided that rather than tolerate delays, they would open the portion to Hay Lane, (officially Wootton Bassett Road), three miles west of Swindon on 17 December 1840, the event being celebrated at Swindon by two brothers, James and Thomas Edwards, giving an exhibition of wrestling and single-stick play. The GWR arranged with the proprietors of the Bath and Bristol stage coaches to work between Hay Lane and Bath, the line from Bristol to Bath having been opened the previous August. Because the highway between Hay Lane and Cirencester was in such a terrible condition that it was virtually impassable, Cheltenham and Gloucester traffic continued to use Faringdon Road as the railhead. Swindon station had yet to be built. The final section of the London-Bristol line, that from Chippenham to Bath and passing through Box Tunnel, was the last to be opened, the date being 30 June 1841. This was not the end of the story for the line was pushed westwards to Penzance, putting Swindon on the main line to the west.

When the Great Western Railway was proposed, it was expected that a branch from Swindon to Cheltenham would be a profitable venture. Directly the GWR bill had been passed by Parliament, some enterprising citizens of Cheltenham produced a scheme for linking their town with the new railway at Swindon. Although only 25 miles separated the two towns as the crow flies, to avoid impossible gradients, the line Brunel surveyed was 44 miles in length and passed through Gloucester and Stroud. Despite opposition from the Thames & Severn Canal and Squire Gordon of Kemble, the Cheltenham & Great Western Union Railway received its Act of Parliament on 21 June 1836. People were slow in subscribing, so it was wisely decided to concentrate on the section between Swindon and Cirencester, as from that railhead coaches could be run to Stroud, Gloucester and Cheltenham. Charles Richardson, a pupil of I. K. Brunel, undertook the supervision and setting out of the line from Swindon to Cirencester. Later he was to design and make the first cricket bat with a spliced cane handle, but was most famous for being chief engineer to the Severn Tunnel.

The opening of the line, expected in January 1841, was delayed by an embankment slipping near Purton, five miles north-west of Swindon. It was found that the core of the bank was saturated and very soft; in fact at one place it subsided 8ft in 24 hours and at another, forced in the side of a cottage. Hoping to cure the trouble Brunel burnt clay on the slopes and filled in the side cuttings where the bank had collapsed, making good the embankment with dry rubble and sand. The CGWUR was opened to Cirencester on 31 May 1841 and the town, instead of being merely at the end of a branch off the Cheltenham line, found itself temporarily the line's main station. Following the arrival of the *Era* coach from Cheltenham, the first train left at 7.15am drawn by the Sharp, Roberts 2-2-2 *Lion* and after waiting at Swindon for about 10 minutes, many of the passengers returned to Cirencester. The opening of the CGWUR had an important effect on the development of Swindon as a rail centre as it made

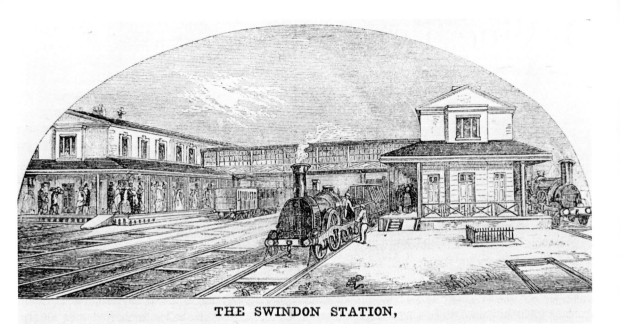

THE SWINDON STATION,

Above: **Swindon Junction, view down c1850.**
George Measom

Swindon a junction where passengers and goods could be interchanged. The CGWUR was taken over by the GWR on 10 May 1844 and for a price of only £230,000, it acquired a partly completed line on which £600,000 had been spent and which had the potentiality of becoming an important through line. The railway from Gloucester to Cheltenham had been opened on 4 November 1840; that from Standish to Gloucester on 8 July 1844 and the section from Kemble to Standish through the 1,864yd long Sapperton Tunnel on 12 May 1845. This meant that Swindon was now connected with the Birmingham & Gloucester Railway, further increasing its importance as a hub of railway activity. The opening of Chepstow Bridge on 19 July 1852 put Swindon on the main line from London to South Wales. The opening of the Severn Tunnel to goods on 1 September 1886 and to passengers three months later, placed Swindon on a more direct line to South Wales.

Although Thingley Junction 19 miles down the line from Swindon was the true junction of the Weymouth branch, the opening of this line with its sea access to and from the Channel Islands, gave an added importance to Swindon. The Wilts, Somerset & Weymouth Railway Act passed on 30 June 1845, authorised a line to be built from the GWR at Thingley to Salisbury, with branches to Weymouth, Devizes, Bradford, Radstock, Sher-

borne and Bridgport, the gauge to be that of the GWR and powers given to lease the line to that company. As so many lines were being projected at the time of the Railway Mania, there was an unusual demand for persons connected with engineering, particularly surveyors and draughtsmen, this shortage delaying the WSWR directors in letting the contracts.

Financial difficulties were also encountered, as owing to the reckless speculation during the Mania, a number of shares had passed into the hands of persons unable to meet calls. The line was eventually opened to Westbury on 5 September 1848; to Frome 7 October 1850 — the first train being an excursion to Oxford via Swindon. There was a long pause before the line reached Yeovil on 1 September 1856, arriving at Weymouth on 15 January the following year. The GWR lost no time in organising trips to Weymouth and by April, cheap excursions ran regularly, arriving on Monday and returning on Saturday, or Saturday week.

Didcot to Swindon was converted to narrow gauge in February 1872 and Swindon to Gloucester on 26 May 1872 for the up line and 29 May for the down line. The conversion of Swindon to Thingley Junction, Chippenham was completed in June 1874. The last broad gauge train to Penzance from Paddington was the 10.15am Cornishman on Friday 20 May 1892 hauled to Bristol by 4-2-2 *Great Western* which arrived Swindon at 11.42 and Penzance 8.20pm instead of its usual time of 6.57. The last up broad

Left: Fire Brand **with down train for Bristol, leaving Swindon 1849. St Mark's Church in background, Gloucester branch right.**
Author's Collection

Right: **Rail routes to Swindon.**

Right: **Mixed gauge turntable for works' trolleys, iron foundry, Swindon Works 24 August 1982.** *Author*

Below: **Last down broad gauge train leaving Swindon Junction 20 May 1892.** *R. H. Cocks*

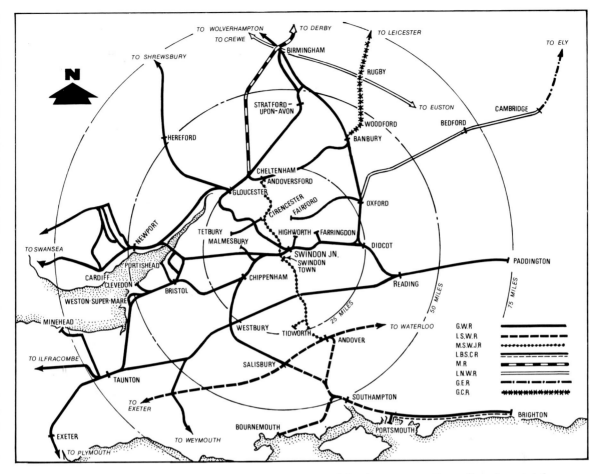

gauge train left Penzance at 9.10pm on 20 May and terminated at Swindon F signalbox at 9.45am on Saturday 21 May. This train called at every station from Penzance to Exeter and Inspector Scantlebury had to receive verbal assurance from each stationmaster personally that no broad gauge vehicles remained in the area under his control.

Commencing 16 May, special trains conveyed broad gauge wagons from west of Exeter to Swindon for conversion or scrap; passenger coaches worked to Swindon on the evening of 20 May in 14 special trains from Penzance, St Erth, Truro, Liskeard, Plymouth and Newton Abbot. The very last broad gauge train to leave Paddington was the 5.00pm Paddington to Plymouth hauled by 4-2-2 *Bulkeley*. The 'Night Mail' leaving at 9.00pm was on the narrow gauge for the first time ever and travelled from Exeter to Plymouth via the LSWR, Cornish mails being carried onwards by steamer.

During the latter half of the last century, people often jokingly remarked that the initials GWR

stood for 'Great Way Round' and certainly many of the Great Western main lines were far from being direct. When the Severn Tunnel was first used, trains from Swindon to South Wales had to curve southwards at Wootton Bassett, pass through Bath and Bristol and then bear northwards to reach the tunnel. Trains were obviously travelling an unnecessary mileage and a new railway was needed between Wootton Bassett and Filton, north of Bristol. The people in South Wales were very dissatisfied with the service provided by the GWR and threatened to build an entirely new line from Cardiff to the London & South Western Railway near Andover. The GWR countered this threat to its traffic by proposing the Bristol & South Wales Direct Railway. This 31-mile long line from Wootton Bassett to Filton had several advantages. It shortened the distance to South Wales by 10 miles; avoided two steep inclines and enabled engines to haul twice the load; shortened the distance from London to Bristol by a mile and relieved the Bathampton to Bristol line on which traffic had greatly increased since the opening of the Severn Tunnel and which could not be easily quadrupled because of the need for heavy engineering works.

The necessary Act of Parliament was passed in August 1896 and the contract for construction let to S. Pearson & Son, it being the largest of its kind to be carried out since the extension of the Great Central Railway to London a few years before. Laid out for ease of running, no gradient on the line was steeper than 1 in 300 and no curve sharper than one mile radius. Considering that the line had to traverse the hilly countryside of the southern Cotswolds, this was a fine achievement. Four of the seven stations had quadruple track so that non-stop trains could by-pass the platforms and most embankments were wide enough to allow for quadrupling throughout. The length of the two tunnels totalled nearly three miles; the three viaducts had 28 arches, while in addition there were 88 bridges. The first through goods train to use the line left Bristol at 8.30am on 1 May 1903; the inaugural passenger train, the 6.32am, running two months later on 1 July.

The other cut-off built by the GWR at the turn of the century and affecting Swindon, was that from Patney to Westbury, and Castle Cary to Langport which provided a direct route from Reading to Taunton avoiding the curve northwards through Didcot and Swindon. As early as 1845 Brunel had planned a railway from Hungerford to Westbury and it was anticipated that eventually Exeter would be reached by a more direct route than via Swindon and Bristol. The aftermath of the Railway Mania made it impossible to raise money, and powers for the line expired before the GWR was able to use them. In 1862 the rather curiously named Berks & Hants Extension Railway opened between Hungerford and Devizes. The BHER did not enter Hampshire, only two miles of its line passed through Berkshire, most of the railway being in Wiltshire!

A line already existed from Devizes through Castle Cary to Weymouth and only 15 miles from Castle Cary was Langport on the Taunton to Yeovil branch, so for the cost of only 15 miles of railway, a new route to the West could be made. Bridges were strengthened, the line doubled and some of the sharper curves on the BHER re-aligned and a cut-off made from Stert to Westbury avoiding the detour via Devizes. The existing line

Below: **Swindon area.**

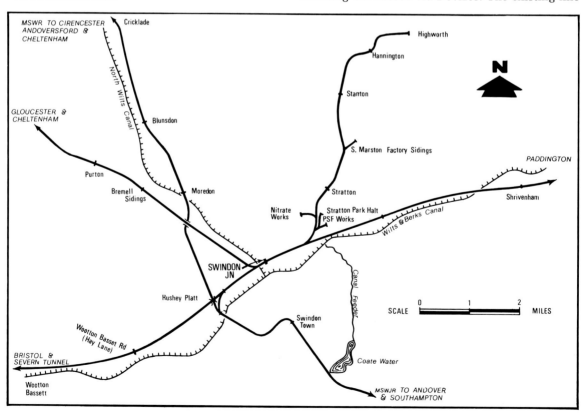

G.W.R.

SWINDON

Above: **Luggage label.**

west of Langport was raised above flood-level and doubled between Curry Rivel Junction and Athelney and a new line built from Athelney to Cogload Junction in order to avoid Durston Junction. This new route was opened to local goods on 2 April 1906, through goods using it on 11 June. It had been planned that express passenger trains to the West of England would be diverted from running via Swindon and use the new line on 2 July, but on the first of the month, a portion of Box Tunnel caved in, so trains were diverted via Castle Cary a day earlier than planned. As it happened, this line was the only one available to the West that day, for the London & South Western line had been blocked at Salisbury by a tragic crash caused when the up boat express from Plymouth travelled at too high a speed round a sharp curve.

The only short branch leaving Swindon was that to Highworth.

Until the Civil War, the town could boast of having the largest market in the whole of Wiltshire, but from that time, traders forsook Highworth for Swindon. Another occurrence affecting the fortunes of the town was the opening of the GWR, this having the effect of taking away all the coaches from the Oxford to Bristol road and causing most of the towns's hotels to close. Highworth felt a strong necessity for a railway — there was the need to despatch agricultural produce and products of the Oriental Matting Company's works in the town and the need of the tradespeople to bring in goods and coal. At a meeting on 8 October 1873 an engineer, Arthur C. Pain was introduced, this gentleman proposing that a light railway be built to Swindon using

powers granted by the Regulation of Railways Act 1868 whereby earthworks and bridge works could be cut to a minimum in return for the introduction of a weight and speed restriction. Pain estimated that costs could be reduced to £4,000 per mile compared wth the £12,305 per mile of the Calne Railway and £10,478 of the Marlborough Railway. The Act of Parliament enabling the Swindon & Highworth Light Railway to be built was passed on 21 June 1875. An agreement was signed with the GWR on 23 December whereby that company would work and maintain the line at 60% of the gross receipts. After this rosy start, the company found that the poor condition of the money market deterred investors, particularly as there was another longer railway being built in the Swindon area — but more about the Swindon, Marlborough & Andover Railway later. Eventually the cash was raised and the ceremony of cutting the first sod performed at Highworth on 6 March 1879, the contractors starting work a fortnight later.

In due course the $5\frac{1}{2}$ miles of 65lb/yd flat bottomed standard gauge rail from Highworth Junction, Swindon to Highworth was complete, or so the company believed, but Colonel Yolland carrying out his Board of Trade inspection on 5 March 1881 thought otherwise. He said that the ballast was mostly sand and only 4-5in deep instead of 12in; points and signals were not interlocked; no locking bars were fitted to the facing points and additional lineside fencing was required. To correct these and other criticisms, the company was required to raise a further sum of £9,000. This left shareholders with the only real option of selling to the GWR which they did on 7 June 1882, receiving only about a fifth of their investment. The GWR spent £18,000 on bringing the line up to standard making the total cost about £79,000, or roughly £14,360 a mile. Major Marindin carried out the re-inspection on 30 April 1883 and passed it. Ceremonial opening of the line was fixed for 8 May, the first train consisting of six first class saloons, four first class compartment stock and four brake coaches which left Highworth at 11.00am behind two locomotives. It arrived at Swindon on schedule at 11.30, returning to Highworth an hour later, while in the afternoon 500 children were taken on a free trip to Swindon and back. Public services began the following day. The branch proved its usefulness, but by 1953, Bristol Tramways & Carriage Company bus services running from the centres of both towns proved more convenient than the stations on the perimeter, so passenger

Above: 253.003 12.35 Swansea-Paddington near Highworth Junction 4 August 1982. *Author*

Left: Class 47 No 47.479 runs light engine off the Highworth branch on 5 April 1974 after taking vans to the BLMC factory. *T. G. Flinders*

Above right: Cutting the first sod of the Swindon, Marlborough & Andover Railway 28 July 1875. *Illustrated London News*

services were withdrawn from 2 March. Workmen's trains continued, but these ceased from 6 August 1962, which meant an end to free travel for people living in Highworth and employed at the Works, the bus fare costing them two shillings and sixpence (12½p) a day. On the same date the branch was closed completely from Kingsdown Road Junction, track being lifted in 1964. 24 June 1965 saw the closure of the line to Stratton, South Marston siding and the Vickers factory north of Milepost 1, the line being curtailed at the north end of the North Sidings beyond the entrance to the Pressed Steel Fisher works.

Although most people regard Swindon as a Great Western centre, it was also an important point on Swindon's other line — the Midland & South Western Junction Railway, being situated midway between Andoversford and Andover. The MSWJR was a cross-country route linking Cheltenham and Southampton, though it never reached either of those towns over its own metals. The MSWJR experienced a chequered history and enjoyed an individuality which persisted long after the original company lost its independence. It was variously known colloquially as the 'Tiddley Dyke', 'Humpty Dumpty' or 'Neddy's Line'. Notwithstanding the fact that it ran through the heart of the GWR countryside, the MSWJR by no means played second fiddle and at one time passengers could travel faster from Cheltenham to London via Andover than more directly in a GWR

train. The MSWJR had its inception during the Railway Mania of 1845, several Manchester to Southampton schemes being proposed and either defeated by finance or the GWR, but the idea of a standard gauge north to south railway cutting across the broad gauge territory remained attractive. Although the Manchester & Southampton scheme failed, its plans were not forgotten and the line gradually developed in a piecemeal fashion. The first section to be built was the Marlborough Railway opened from Savernake on 14 April 1864, followed by the Andover & Redbridge Railway on 6 March 1865. In 1864 John Sewell, a London engineer, proposed the Gloucester, Wilts & Hants, or the Great North & South Junction Railway. His intention was to use the Midland Railway from the north to Gloucester; the GWR to Swindon; a new line built onwards to Marlborough where the Marlborough Railway would carry trains to Savernake; another new line being built to connect with Andover; the Andover & Redbridge Railway giving access to Southampton. The Act of the Swindon, Marlborough & Andover Railway as it was called, received Royal Assent 21 July 1873. The ceremony of turning the first turf took place on 28 July 1875 at Marlborough, William Wright, the contractor, starting work on a costly 773yd long tunnel at Swindon by the present Queen's Gardens which the *Swindon Advertiser* claimed could have been avoided by approaching Swindon Junction from the west instead of the east.

Cost of the Tunnel Route

	£
Earthworks — 351,000cu yd	17,550
Tunnel	42,500
Bridges (6)	4,650
Diversion of roads	370
Contingencies 15%	9,750
	74,820

Cost of the route proposed by the 'Swindon Advertiser'

	£
Earthworks — 176,000cu yd	8,800
Bridges (6)	4,650
Diversion of roads	370
Contingencies 10%	1,380
	15,200

Difference: £59,620

Wright proved a wrong choice by going bankrupt and the directors looking round for economies as shares were slow to be taken up, adopted the *Swindon Advertiser* route. Eventually money was raised and the tenders of Messrs Watson, Smith, Watson Ltd signed on 29 August 1879. Colonel Yolland in inspecting the line from Marlborough to Swindon on 20 July 1880, suggested several minor improvements and paid tribute to the solidarity of the bridges. As the ceremony of turning the first sod had taken place at Marlborough, it was agreed that the opening celebrations would be held at Swindon. The directors travelled from Swindon to Marlborough to meet the Marquess of Ailesbury and the mayor and corporation of Marlborough who boarded the special. It arrived detonating fog signals at Old Town station, Swindon. The Town Band in their gay red and blue uniforms led the gentry to a banquet at the Corn Exchange. Public traffic began on 27 July.

Although the SMAR brought its rails close to the GWR at Rushey Platt, the latter company failed to lay the junction even though the Act gave the SMAR running powers. People commented on the different treatment afforded the Swindon & Highworth Light Railway with which a junction was made long before its rails were ready. Even when the junction was put in at Rushey Platt and passed by the Board of Trade on 20 October 1881, it remained unused owing to a lack of agreement as to whether the SMAR should work to Swindon Junction, or the GWR to Swindon Town. Eventually the SMAR assented to run its passen-

REFERENCE

Midland & South Western Junction Railway.

REFERENCE TO

YOUR LETTER.

Memo. from
GENERAL MANAGER'S OFFICE,
CIRENCESTER 14-1- 189

To Mr Bowyer
Rushey Platt.

L & S W wagon 7549. Oct 16 to 21/03.
1 day 3/-

Please say if the above amount has been collected. If not let me have full explanation of the detention to the vehicle, with copy of entry.

JOHN DAVIES
SAM FAY.

Right: **Swindon Junction cabin (junction with MSWJR at Rushey Platt) c1890. Gloucester Carriage & Wagon Co signalbox, GWR frame.**
Gloucester Carriage & Wagon Co

Below left: **MSWJR form for demurrage of LSWR wagon at Rushey Platt.**

ger trains into the GWR station on 6 February 1882. The GWR calculated tolls on a notional distance of six miles from Rushey Platt to Swindon Junction, instead of the actual distance of 1 mile 18 chains. It demanded a minimum payment of £900 per annum, plus £1,500 for the use of the station and an additional £5,000 to £6,000 for an easement to make a junction at Rushey Platt. These outrageous terms were reduced by arbitration to a much more reasonable notional distance of two miles, with a minimum of £200 annually for the tolls; £900 for the use of Swindon Junction station and £105 for the junction easement. Even with these reduced payments, the service proved unprofitable to the SMAR as most passengers required a journey either to or from Swindon Town, rather than rail travel beyond. As the service lost the company nearly £1,500 annually, it was withdrawn on 28 February 1885.

Major Marindin of the Board of Trade inspected the line from Savernake to Andover on 21 March 1882. Although the line was satisfactory, he found the Berks & Hants station at Savernake unsuitable to take extra traffic, also insisting that the block telegraph be installed on the Marlborough Railway. In order to make some profit on their investment, the SMAR directors decided to open the Grafton to Andover section on 1 May. Matters having been corrected, the whole line was ceremonially opened on 3 February 1883, guests leaving Swindon Town at 10.40am

and arriving Andover 12.20pm. Public opening was on 5 February. The *Swindon Advertiser* noted in its editorial that when the GWR had been the sole railway in the town it 'charged the utmost farthing for the accommodation it has afforded; but when there has been competition, when other railway systems have contended with it for the trade and patronage of a town or district, then the Great Western had lowered its rates and extended its facilities in a very marked manner'.

The success of the SMAR depended on an independent extension being built to the Midland Railway so that it would be on a through route. The Swindon & Cheltenham Extension Railway was planned to run northwards from the SMAR at Rushey Platt to Andoversford on the Banbury & Cheltenham Railway, over which running powers would be used. The SCER Act was passed on 18 July 1881, Watson, Smith,Watson beginning the contract the following April. Meanwhile the GWR had leased the Didcot & Newbury line and tried petty methods to stop north to south opposition. The SCER offered to pay £210 for an easement to cross the Great Western's Cheltenham line near Moredon as its Act authorised, but the GWR countered this by invoking the Land Clauses Act of 1845 which provided that a company could not take land until the whole of its capital was subscribed. The SCER appealed as the intention of the 1845 Act was to protect a landowner against having his land taken from him by a railway

Right: **Former MSWJR offices at Swindon Town 17 April 1961.** *Author*

when there was a probability it would not be made. The Master of the Rolls gave judgement in favour of the SCER, the GWR's appeal to the House of Lords being rejected.

The line between Rushey Platt and Cirencester was opened to goods traffic on 1 November 1883 and to passengers on 18 December. By an Act of 23 June 1884 the SMAR and the SCER were amalgamated to form the Midland & South Western Junction Railway. The company's financial affairs were so critical that drastic economies had to be made such as withdrawing the Swindon Junction service, reducing that to Cirencester and pruning staff. In November the contractors were released and went bankrupt the following year. On 20 December 1884 Lt Col Francis Douglas Grey, the MSWJR's deputy chairman was appointed Receiver in Chancery. In May 1888 the contractor Charles Braddock began work on the extension from Cirencester to Andoversford, the line being inspected by Major Marindin on 23/24 January 1891 and opened to goods traffic 16 March, passenger traffic starting on 1 August. The MSWJR anticipating more through traffic via Cheltenham and less via Swindon, it informed the GWR that on and after 1 August 1891 it would cease running goods trains into Swindon Junction station and no longer pay the expenses of Rushey Platt Junction signalbox, all traffic being exchanged at Rushey Platt sidings.

Sam Fay, appointed general manager of the MSWJR for a period of five years from 1 February 1892, took positive steps to re-vitalise the line and utilise its great possibilities. So successful was Fay that the company was taken out of the Court of Chancery on 27 May 1897. With increasing receipts as the company went all-out to obtain

traffic, various improvements could be made such as an independent line from Marlborough to Grafton and much of the single line doubled. During both world wars the railway provided the country with a vital lifeline taking strategic materials from the Midlands to the south coast and wounded from Southampton northwards. The MSWJR was absorbed by the GWR on 1 July 1923 being the biggest subsidiary, as distinct from constituent company, to be absorbed as part of the Great Western. The GWR made various economies, the MSWJR headquarters at Swindon Town being closed in 1924 as was the locomotive, carriage and wagon works at Cirencester and the Swindon Town engine shed; its stud being transferred to Swindon Junction. Track changes at Lansdown Junction, Cheltenham, robbed MSWJR trains of the route into the Midland station and on 3 November 1958 the surviving train was diverted into Cheltenham St James. As this effectively denuded the line of its through traffic, and as the number of local passengers were insufficient to justify trains being run, services over the whole line were withdrawn from 9 September 1961 and some sections, including Marlborough to Swindon Town and Cirencester to Andoversford, closed completely. The diesel hauled goods train which ran from Mondays to Fridays between Swindon and Cirencester was withdrawn from 1 April 1964, but coal trains continued to work as required to Moredon power station, mainly in winter as the station was only a stand-by. This traffic came to an end when it was closed in 1973. The line saw a brief resurgence when it was used to carry road materials to Swindon Town for building the M4 Motorway, but was eventually closed, track being lifted from Moredon and Swindon Town in 1978.

Development of Passenger Services

Main Line

Swindon was an important station because a condition of the lease stipulated that all trains carrying passengers were to stop for 10 minutes in order to give passengers an opportunity to buy refreshments. The timetable for 30 July 1841 showed nine down and the same number of up trains daily, mail trains covering the distance of 77 miles from Paddington in 155min. Four trains ran each way on Sundays, with seven to and from Cirencester on weekdays and three on Sundays. On 10 March 1845 the Exeter train was speeded to 110min from Paddington to Swindon; 12 May 102min, 26 January 1846 98min and December 1847 85min — these trains easily being the fastest in the world. For the 52.7 miles from the old terminus at Paddington to Didcot only 55min were allowed, involving an average speed of over 57mile/h and on 11 May 1848 it is recorded that the 4-2-2 *Great Britain* covered the distance in 47$\frac{1}{2}$min. In 1849 this train was nicknamed the 'Flying Dutchman' after a horse which that year won both the Derby and the St Leger. Up expresses of the period were not quite so speedy, though one ran from Swindon to Didcot in 27min, averaging rather more than 53$\frac{1}{2}$mile/h. From 1852 onwards, speed on the Great Western was in

Weekdays — through trains from Swindon to:

	July 1854	July 1914	July 1939	July 1960
London	10	14	24	19
Bristol (inclusive via Badminton)	10	19	28	22
Cardiff via Gloucester	NK	6	4	2
Cardiff via Severn Tunnel	Nil	12	13	11
Highworth	Nil	7	3	0
Southampton MSWJR	Nil	4	2	1
Cheltenham MSWJR	Nil	7	4	1

the doldrums, but in 1862 under the spur of London & South Western Railway competition, the down 'Flying Dutchman' was speeded to 90min and two years later the Didcot stop was omitted, the 77.3 miles still booked to be covered in 90min as drivers could not, or perhaps for coal economy reasons, would not, keep time to

Below: **10.30am Paddington-Plymouth passing Swindon, 1 October 1895.**
Collection: Sean Bolan

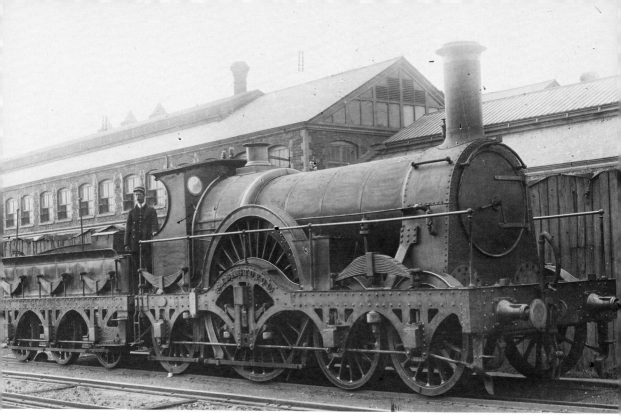

Above: Sebastopol at **Swindon. Engine similar to** *Great Britain.* **LPC**

Below: **'B1' 4-6-0 No 61183 at Swindon Junction after arrival of a Sheffield train. No 6994** *Baggrave Hall* **on right. 19 February 1961.** *L. Sandler*

Swindon. Normal formation of the 'Flying Dutchman' was seven six-wheeled coaches from Paddington to Swindon where two were detached: one for Weymouth and another for Cheltenham. The train was further accelerated in 1871 to 87min and when the 'Cornishman' began in the summer of 1890, it was also scheduled to take 87min.

In the 1880s South Wales expresses in addition to coaches for Swansea and New Milford, also had carriages for Cheltenham and Weymouth, some even having Bristol and Hereford portions as well, these being detached and re-marshalled at Swindon. In 1880 the fastest narrow gauge train from Paddington to Swindon was the 5.15pm South Wales express, which reached Swindon at 7.10pm after having stopped at Reading for 5min. Up narrow gauge expresses were faster than the down, the best consisting of portions from Cheltenham and Bristol combined at Swindon. Departing at 9.05am it arrived Reading 9.55, left at 10am and reached Paddington at 10.45. One up train in addition to the South Wales and Bristol portions giving a combined weight in excess of 160 tons, also had tail traffic of half a dozen six-wheeled milk vans making a total of 260 tons. In the mid-1880s, one or two standard gauge trains ran non-stop Paddington to Swindon, the New Milford Boat Train covering the distance in 97min and 10min slower than the fastest broad gauge express, an average of 47.8miles/h. Its load was at least 150 tons, frequently exceeded 200 tons and could not have held to an 87min schedule, but the 10.50am standard gauge Swindon to Paddington with less than 100 tons behind the tender could have kept this schedule if allowed to, but perhaps the reason it was not speeded up was because it conveyed third class passengers. Until 1890 this was the only standard gauge express from Exeter and Bristol, as opposed to just coaches from Bristol attached at Swindon to a South Wales train. In 1887 the 10.25am ex-Paddington was divided at Swindon into two portions: the leading one via Bath, Stapleton Road to New Milford, while the rear portion ran to Weymouth.

By August 1887 Swindon was served by 19 down and 17 up trains. This was the year a new broad gauge express ran in each direction to Plymouth. Called the 'Jubilee', it conveyed third class passengers and was timed 95min non-stop to Swindon compared with the 87min of the expresses conveying first and second class passengers only. In the 1880s the 'Flying Dutchman' had a minimum load of five eight-wheeled coaches,

frequently six and occasionally seven; the 'Zulu', which ran in the afternoon, rarely had more than five. Broad gauge engines could only keep time from Paddington to Swindon with six coaches if there was no head wind. Drivers had little incentive to keep time as the Swindon to Bristol run was booked at 47mile/h and a few minutes lost east of Swindon could easily be made up down Wootton Bassett and Box Tunnel banks of 1 in 100. E. L. Ahrons said that up trains kept time and covered the distance from Swindon to Paddington in 85min.

In 1891 the 3.10pm South Wales express covered the distance to Swindon in 90min at an average speed of $51\frac{1}{2}$mile/h — the fastest standard gauge timing to date, the same year an up express from South Wales ran to the same timing. In 1895 nine daily services ran from Paddington to Swindon at an average speed of $53\frac{1}{4}$mile/h with loads varying from five to 10 eight-wheeled coaches. In 1901 there were nine slip coach workings to and from Swindon: the 7.50am express ex-Bristol slipped a coach at Swindon in connection with the 9.02am express from Swindon to Paddington which in its turn conveyed slip coaches for Reading, Didcot and Oxford, the latter carrying Great Central Railway passengers via Banbury. The 9am, 11.45am and 3pm expresses from Paddington had slip coaches attached at Swindon for Chippenham and Weymouth and the 10.15am and the 4.20pm slip coaches for Oxford and Didcot respectively, these two latter trains being expresses from Weymouth. A further slip was attached to the 4.58pm the up 'Jubilee'. In the late 1920s, two up trains slipped coaches at Swindon, the actual point of slipping being under the MSWJR bridge, the station pilot drawing them into the platform.

On 20 April 1905 the Great Central Railway operated a 374-mile excursion from Manchester to Plymouth via Swindon with 4-4-2 No 267, this being the longest record for through running and was held until the LMS and the LNER ran through locomotives from London to Scotland. From Newton Abbot the GCR locomotive was assisted by a GWR engine. The excursion was repeated on 12 April 1906. On 16 September 1907 the GWR performed the longest GWR non-stop run of $261\frac{1}{2}$ miles with a special from Paddington to Fishguard, 4-4-0 No 3408 *Ophir* hauling a train of 200 tons, passed Swindon in 76min 16sec. In April 1910 14 down and 16 up trains were run Swindon to Paddington, while on weekdays was a train from Nottingham (Victoria) on the GCR, to Weston-super-Mare via Swindon and a return from Bristol to Nottingham. In October 1921 the GCR introduced through trains Aberdeen to Penzance, departing Aberdeen 9.45am and arriving at Penzance 7.40am the next day, the sleeping car being attached at Swindon. The up train left Penzance at 11.10am and arrived Aberdeen 7.40am.

In 1923 the GWR decided to claim the railway speed record in Great Britain held by the North Eastern Railway so accelerated the 'Cheltenham Flyer' to 75min for its journey from Swindon to Paddington; in July 1929 to 70min requiring an average speed of 66.2mile/h; September 1931 to 67min bringing the average to 69.2mile/h and finally in September 1932 to 65min-71.4mile/h, its best recorded journey made on 6 June 1932 when the 77.3 miles were covered in 56min 47sec, at an average of 81.7mile/h by 4-6-0 No 5006 *Tregenna Castle* with a load of six bogie coaches. As critics said that performance was due to the route being 'all downhill', on the same date the *down* 'Cheltenham Spa Express' was also run at high speed, the 5.00pm from Paddington being specially stopped at Swindon for direct comparison as it was not a scheduled halt, No 5005 *Manorbier Castle* covering the distance in 60min 1sec.

The 'Merchant Venturer' introduced May 1951 ran non-stop Paddington to Bath, but made several intermediate stops in the up direction,

Paddington being reached in 105min including a stop at Reading. The title disappeared in the 1965 timetable re-organisation.

The Little Somerford to Malmesbury branch had a through return train from Malmesbury to Swindon on Thursday and Saturday evenings until closure on 10 September 1951; the stopping service Bristol to Swindon via Little Somerford was withdrawn 3 April 1961; stopping services to Didcot on 7 December 1964 and Bristol to Swindon via Bath 4 January 1965.

Because the AC Cars four-wheeled railbuses on the Cirencester and Tetbury branches were too light to operate the track circuits on the main line reliably, they were not allowed to carry passengers through to Swindon. In March 1967 the 'Bristol Pullman' stopped at Swindon in the up direction giving, with a stop at Reading, a time to

Below: **No 5001** *Llandovery Castle* **passing Swindon Junction with down express 4 April 1946.**
H. C. Casserley

Right: **Up 'Bristol Pullman' overtaking a train hauled by a 'Western' class diesel-hydraulic at Swindon 1969.**
BR

Below right: **Unloading the 12.40 Paddington-Bristol at Swindon, 2 June 1982.** *Author*

Above: Class 47 No D1642 nears Highworth Junction with a Swansea-Paddington service, February 1969. *T. G. Flinders*

Paddington of 80min. The introduction of Mark 2 coaches caused the 'Blue Pullmans' to have little appeal, so they were taken out of service in the spring of 1973. From 1975 pre-production HST No 252.001 ran on various trains to Swindon at conventional speeds. HSTs were introduced on 4 October 1976 knocking 20min off the run from Paddington the distance being covered in 49min.

The Borough of Thamesdown has an aggressive policy of bringing new business to Swindon and has been successful in attracting firms — being able to offer lower office rates than London and a good connection with the metropolis by road and rail. The population of Swindon rose from the 1971 figure of 161,000 to 177,000 in 1981, the projected figure for 1991 being 203-311,000. The establishment of offices of various companies at Swindon has made passenger business flourish, the volume having risen by a third in the years

1977-82, sales of season tickets doubling during this period. Passengers from Swindon mainly travel to London and quite a few to Heathrow. There is an interchange from expresses to Cheltenham DMUS, especially since early 1981 when some Cheltenham to Paddington expresses were withdrawn forcing more passengers to change at Swindon, but there is not much interchange from up trains to the Cheltenham line. In 1982-3 24 trains ran from Swindon to Bristol Temple Meads and nine from Swindon to South Wales with 30 trains Swindon to Paddington. Seventeen run each way to and from Gloucester providing roughly an hourly service, mostly DMU operated, but with two locomotive hauled trains in each direction, occasionally worked by HSTs. The 13.10 Paignton to Paddington runs via Swindon and two run in the opposite direction. The fastest postwar steam service Swindon to Paddington was 79min, the fastest HST 47min down and 49 up. 13 July 1981 a Swindon-Westbury-Weymouth service was operated Mondays to Thursdays during the school holidays, running by local arrangement. It was successful and on fine days the 'Weymouth Wizard' arrived at the resort with 500 passengers.

Weekdays — through trains from Swindon to:

	1854	July 1914	July 1939	July 1960	January 1983
London	10	14	24	19	33
Bristol (inclusive via Badminton)	10	19	28	22	27
Cardiff via Gloucester	NK	6	4	2	0
Cardiff via Severn Tunnel	0	12	13	11	14
Highworth	0	7	3	0	0
Southampton MSWJR	0	4	2	1	0
Cheltenham MSWJR	0	7	4	1	0

	1914	1939	1947	1961	1973	1974	1983
Fastest in minutes	84	65	85	79	65	69	47
No through to Paddington	13	17	11	21	26	27	32
No through to Paddington before 11am (commuter growth)	2	2	2	3	6	7	10

Below : **Down 'Capitals United' express behind No D1699, September 1965.** *J. D. Benson*

Trains mainly for the benefit of employees of Swindon Works ran morning and evening, from Cirencester (Watermoor), Highworth, Shrivenham, Chiseldon, Wootton Bassett and Purton, though they were also available to the general public. The evening train serving Purton was extended to Kemble where it connected with the Tetbury and Cirencester (Town) branches and also with a push-pull auto train to Chalford. The train from Watermoor was interesting in that workers were conveyed to Swindon Town station where 5min was allowed to change to the train from Chiseldon which took them to Swindon Junction. It was not unknown for workmen's trains to reach speeds of 60-70mile/h on the main line from Shrivenham, Wootton Bassett and Purton, drivers trying to be the first to arrive at Swindon Junction. During the years before the Depression, a significant percentage of men who had completed their apprenticeship at the Works and not able to be given a permanent job, were employed at Morris Motors, Cowley, the GWR running a special workmen's train for them to and from Oxford daily.

The Highworth branch service started with five down and five up trains, plus an additional up train on Mondays, Swindon market day. Trains took 30min for the 6½ miles, except the first down and last up which were mixed and took 50 and 45 minutes respectively. A workmen's service started in January 1890 left Highworth at 5.20am. In the evening the 5.0pm from Swindon (5.55pm return) was discontinued and replaced by two workings: the 4.35pm (5.05pm return) and 5.45pm (6.20pm return). The 5.05pm from Highworth ran nonstop back to Swindon in order to form the 5.45pm. Workmen's trains, although stopping at Swindon Junction for ordinary passengers, worked through to a timber platform near Swindon G signalbox, latterly named Loco Yard. By 1900 a Sunday service was operated, probably mainly to deal with milk traffic. The timetable for April 1900 showed five each way plus an extra each way on Mondays. Two ran in each direction on Sundays. After the branch had closed to passengers on 2 March 1953, the Mondays to Fridays workmen's trains continued to run departing Highworth 6.47am and arriving Swindon Junction 7.14am, the return working at 5.56pm arriving Highworth 6.27pm. Due to the fuel shortage during the Suez Crisis of 1956, a workmen's train was run for Vickers' South Marston employees on 17 December departing Swindon Junction 7.38am, arriving Vickers' platform 7.50. The platform had been built for workers in World War 2. Two return evening trains were run on some days and also one on Sunday. The last of these trains to Vickers ran on 30 June 1957. Trains consisted of up to eight eight-wheeled clerestory vehicles which were able to run to the factory as bridges had been rebuilt to accommodate the standard loading gauge, but the Highworth 'B' set had to be specially made with ventilators well down the roof instead of near the apex. On the outbreak of World War 2 in 1939, the 'B' set was temporarily replaced by wooden seated four-wheeled coaches mostly used for South Wales miners' trains.

GWR Buses

From 31 May to 5 June 1906 the GWR ran a bus service from the station to the Bath & West showground using at least two buses which were presumably parked somewhere near the station. However an outing from the Works a few years later used Bath Electric Tramways buses! From 2 October 1911 until 29 September 1913 GWR buses ran into Swindon from the south on two or three days a week depending on the timetable. The small Dennis buses were stationed at Aldbourne. On 17 October 1924 a service commenced between Swindon and Wantage Road station, buses being garaged at Swindon and a Swindon to Lambourn service started on 17 August 1925. There were variations to the routes, nearly all villages on the edge of the downs being served. The final service in the area was from Swindon to Banbury via Burford inaugurated on 1 July 1929, worked from both ends.

Originally buses worked from Harding's Yard at Gorse Hill, Swindon and others were outstationed at various times at Lambourn, Uffington and the Rose & Crown, Ashbury. Eventually Wantage became the main depot for the passenger services, Swindon concentrating on goods and parcels, becoming an outstation for passenger services.

MSWJR

The *Marlborough Times* of 16 July 1881 reported: 'In daily expectation of the visit of the Inspector of the Board of Trade, a train service has been running experimentally on this line. Five trains have been started each way, stopping at Chiseldon and Ogbourne stations, and the journey between Marlborough and Old Swindon has in

Above: **Station offices at Swindon Junction. Notice projecting ticket office. GWR bus registration AF 71.** *GWR*

every case been accomplished in 25 minutes. Trains have been loaded with passengers (primarily from Swindon) for these gratuitous trips, and everything has run smoothly and well'. Profit-making services began 27 July with six trains daily each way from Swindon Town to Marlborough and two on Sundays taking about 30min for the distance of $11\frac{1}{4}$ miles. The time allowance was found to be inadequate and from the following month, trains were given an extra 5min. An additional late train ran each way on Saturdays. On the first Bank Holiday, the railway cancelled ordinary services and special trains were run at intervals of $1\frac{1}{2}$hr, principally carrying trippers to Marlborough where they walked to Savernake Forest for picnics; of the 1,400 passengers carried, 950 booked from Swindon.

With the opening of the extension to Swindon Junction on 6 February 1882, six trains ran through from Marlborough taking about 40min, one each way terminating at Swindon Town. When the line was opened through to Andover and Southampton, seven trains ran from Swindon, all but two starting from Swindon Junction, the seven up trains all running through to the GWR station. Two trains ran each way on

Sundays from Swindon Town to Cirencester. Services commenced with five trains each way and two on Sundays taking about 30min for the trip; the first train of the day left from Rushey Platt, the remainder from Swindon Town. For the opening to Cheltenham in 1891, three trains ran each way, soon increased to four down from Cheltenham and five up, one of the latter being mixed. The principal MSWJR trains were called the North Express and the South Express.

Through coaches started in the summer of 1893 running daily from Bradford, Leeds, Sheffield, Derby, Liverpool, Birmingham and Southampton, the MSWJR providing the shortest route. Through coaches also ran from Cheltenham to Portsmouth. By August 1898 through services between Cheltenham and Andover had increased to six down and five up trains with an additional each way on Saturdays. Two through up trains were run on Sundays, but none in the reverse direction. In May 1911 through coaches ran between Southampton and Nottingham, Birmingham, Manchester, Stockport and Crewe. August 1914 marked the peak of MSWJR services, with weekend trains of eight or nine coaches. Two South Expresses were run to Southampton: one from Birmingham, the other from Manchester (London Road). World War 1 caused the cessation of through carriages and when resumed in 1922, the Southampton to Manchester coach had been diverted to Liverpool and the second through service reduced to a semi-fast between Cheltenham and Southampton. The last MSWJR time-table issued July 1923 showed four through trains each way.

On 22 October 1923 the GWR restored the Swindon Town-Swindon Junction shuttle service, only to discontinue it 21 September 1925 and reinstate it within six months. The working was colloquially known as the 'Old Town Bunk', 'Dodger', or 'Loop' train. It was run entirely for the convenience of long-distance passengers, the rail mileage being $3\frac{1}{2}$ as opposed to $1\frac{1}{2}$ miles by tram, the latter being cheaper. The train was a great favourite of loco spotters since it enabled them to see new engines outside the works. On 6 April 1936 a supplementary diesel railcar service was introduced running Cheltenham St James, Swindon Town, Swindon Junction, Swindon Town, Cheltenham St James, Swindon Town, Savernake, Devizes, Swindon Town, Swindon Junction, Stroud, Gloucester and Cheltenham St James. Though it provided a fast service reaching 60mile/h in places, it was soon withdrawn through lack of traffic.

The GWR continued the through coach from Liverpool, Lime Street to Southampton until the beginning of World War 2 when there were still four through trains between Cheltenham and Andover. From 1 October 1941 the 2.00pm Cheltenham to Andover, the old South Express and the 2.35 Andover to Cheltenham were withdrawn. They were restored in 1946 making four through trains each way until the winter time-table of 1951 when the 2.35 from Andover was curtailed at Swindon Town, returning at 4.48 in place of the 3.05 ex-Cheltenham. Three of the Swindon Town to Andover services were also withdrawn that winter. A drastic cut on 30 June 1958 reduced the number of through trains from three to one, this lasting until the line's closure.

Apart from regular services, various specials were run. From July 1893 an Ocean Boat Express ran from various places in the north to South-ampton via Swindon Town and continued until 1914. Another train carried emigrants from Liver-pool to Southampton every Friday morning, some-times being so heavy that it was required to run in two portions; from July to September 1913, $2,891\frac{1}{2}$ emigrants were carried. Every Tuesday and Friday an express to the docks was provided for passengers travelling by the American Lines and White Star Lines to New York and by the Union Castle boats to the Cape, the train stopping for ocean-going passengers at any MSWJR station on 24 hours notice.

Below: **Train for ex-MSWJR line at Swindon Junction, 3 September 1961, hauled by No 5306.** *D. J. Hyde*

Trip week

One of the features of the Works was the annual Trip during the first week in July — earlier than most factories elsewhere in order that locomotives would not be taken from paying passengers at the height of the season a few weeks later. The majority of locomotives used on the Trip trains were stock engines, that is locomotives recently released from the works; the coaches came from the carriage store at Newburn. The Trip started in 1849 when 500 workmen travelled to Oxford by special train. It developed through the years and in 1908 no less than 24,564 were carried from Swindon in the early morning by 22 special trains before most of the ordinary traffic started. Weymouth, or 'Swindon-by-the-Sea' was highly popular, 6,171 arriving at this destination; other specials ran to London, Weston-super-Mare, Winchester, South Wales and the West and North of England. Two trains ran to Southsea via the MSWJR, these consisting of LSWR stock hauled by a 'T9' 4-4-0 which always ran tender first with empty stock, even though it could be turned at Swindon. To ease congestion, Trip trains left from various parts of the Works, portable steps being used. In 1913 the Trip was extended to a whole week. In 1939 27,000 left Swindon in 30 special trains. On Wednesdays shops closed at lunchtime,

Above: **No 7741 arriving at Swindon Town with 11.13am from Swindon Junction 6 December 1952.** *Hugh Ballantyne*

but during Trip Week they closed for the whole of the day, practically everyone going off and leaving Swindon like a ghost town. On the following Friday evening, Trip trains arrived back at Swindon. Trip Week was really a lock out for the workmen until a week's paid holiday was given in 1938, extended to a fortnight 10 years later. With the increase in car ownership, numbers using the Trip trains dwindled until they stopped in 1960, ordinary services being able to cope with the numbers, but in 1976 BR said it 'arranged one or two special trains because there were enough employees going to the same place to justify it'.

Well within living memory children with prams and four-wheel 'bogies' transported luggage to the station from quite a distance for a couple of pence while the owners walked, few buses running in connection with trip trains. The favourite accommodation away was 'room and attendance' where the tripper would supply the food for the landlady to prepare, some families even taking their own vegetables.

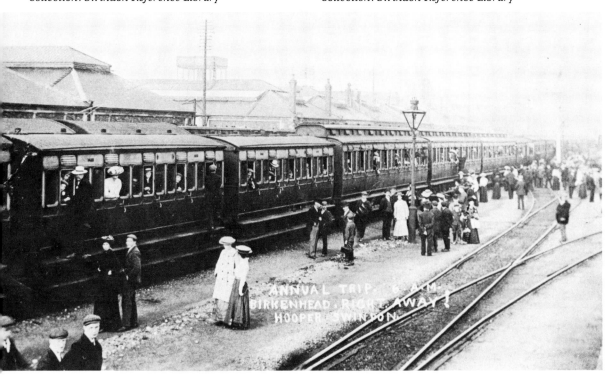

Development of Freight Services

The story of freight services at Swindon is very much a tale of development and a traumatic reduction. With the opening of the line to Bristol in 1841, two goods trains were run daily in each direction 15-20min being allowed at Swindon for shunting. At first traffic would have been closely allied to the Works, or local tradesmen; then, as the British railway network developed, so did freight traffic at Swindon. As canal traffic declined, rail traffic increased. Locomotive coal instead of being carried by canal, was brought by rail. In the 1880s, the 'Broad Gauge Tip' worked by 2-4-0 Nos 2015-2024 ex-Bristol & Exeter Railway engines and shedded at Bristol, hauled this train between Reading and Swindon at a very respectable average of 33miles/h and from Swindon to Bristol at 35.3mile/h. Although with their 6ft 6in wheels they were really passenger engines, because they were prone to rough riding, they were normally kept for fast goods such as this. In the 1880s footplate crews worked long hours, one turn involved leaving Swindon at 4.48pm, the goods engine piloting the heavy Hereford, Cheltenham and Swansea express to Stroud, where it waited for the Aberdare coal train which had left Swindon earlier that afternoon. This train arrived in Gloucester about 7.00pm. The goods engine worked the 9.15pm Gloucester to Newport consisting of two six-wheeled coaches and goods brake van stopping only at Lydney and Chepstow. From Newport the engine and brake ran light to Rogerstone Sidings, (then known as Tydu) and coupled to a heavy coal train departed at 2.00am arriving at Swindon between 6.00am and 8.00am. Most Aberdare to Swindon coal trains worked the distance of 108 miles by 0-6-0STs of the '1260' and '1581' classes shedded at Aberdare. In 1901 no less than 144 goods and mineral trains were booked daily to stop at Swindon and take on, put off, or exchange traffic, compared with only 66 such trains in 1873.

One of the industries associated with Swindon as a railway centre was J. Compton Sons & Webb Ltd who made uniforms in 1848 for the Great Western and other railways, the police and Post Office; other clothing manufacturers in the town being Nicholson's raincoats and the Cellular Clothing Company. There was also Garrard's gramophone and electrical equipment works. In 1916 the Ministry of Munitions set up Stratton Filling Factory for making ammonium nitrate on the west side of the Highworth branch near its junction with the main line. Served by standard gauge sidings which were opened 18 February 1917 and closed 28 July 1919, there was also a narrow gauge system.

Below: **No 7914** *Lleweni Hall* **and 'ROD' No 3047 on up goods train passing Swindon Junction 22 June 1952.** *W. Potter*

Standard gauge locomotives at Stratton Filling Factory

No		Works No	Date built
—	0-6-0ST Manning, Wardle	1943	1917
—	0-6-0T Kerr, Stuart	3078	1917
101	0-4-0T LSW, Eastleigh	—	1910*
—	0-6-0ST Avonside	1016	1874†
—	0-6-0ST Hunslet	468	1888‡

*Ex-LSWR 'S14' class motor tank No 101
†Ex-Neath & Brecon Railway No 4
‡Ex-Price, Wills & Reeves, contractors. This locomotive is believed to have worked at Swindon.

2ft gauge

Four-wheeled battery powered electric locomotive built Brush c1917 works Nos 16296/7/8.

The ammonium nitrate was transported about 300yd by aerial ropeway to the ammunition factory, now W. D. & H. O. Wills' tobacco works. About 60 wagons of ammunition left the factory daily during World War 1. Between July 1920 and September 1921 50 Railway Operating Division 2-8-0 locomotives were brought to Stratton Filling Factory sidings from the GWR, GCR and LSWR for storage until transferred to the GWR in May 1925. The War Department used the factory site as No 4 Supply Reserve Depot until about 1960, the sidings being worked by standard WD locomotives. The northern part of the works became the Plessey factory to which sidings were opened 24 June 1941. To overcome a possible conflicting movement from the Supply Reserve Depot and Plessey sidings, before shunting into the latter, the guard or shunter placed a red flag in daytime, or a red light at night on each of the two flag boards, this banning shunting on Supply Reserve Depot sidings. Plessey ground frame renamed Green Lane 'B' on 1 April 1959, was taken out of use 13 July 1966. Stratton ground frame opened circa July 1941 giving access to the Supply Reserve Depot, was renamed Green Lane 'A' on 1 April 1959 and taken out of use 13 November 1964. A locomotive was authorised, to propel up to 30 wagons from the Transfer Yard to the Supply Reserve Depot sidings except during fog or falling snow. A manned brake van was required to be at the head of the rake, speed was limited to 10mile/h, with a lower limit of 4mile/h over facing points and crossings. The same rule applied to Pressed Steel Fisher sidings, but a brake van was not necessary.

Moredon power station situated on the east side of the MSWJR line north of the point where it passed under the Cheltenham line and served by sidings, opened to traffic 17 January 1928. Before 1962 most of the coal used came from the Forest of Dean, but as the supply from that source decreased, East Midlands coal was substituted and in 1963 the four low pressure boilers were converted to burn oil. No 1, a four-wheeled petrol shunter was scrapped about 1941 and replaced by No 2, a four-wheeled battery-electric locomotive built by English Electric, works No 1197, with mechanical parts by Andrew Barclay. This ran until the power station closed in 1973. The locomotive was stabled in the workshops.

W. D. & H. O. Wills' cigarette and tobacco works at Colbourne Street near the GWR goods shed had standard gauge sidings worked by a four-wheeled petrol engine Muir Hill locomotive, works No 27 of 1927, replaced in 1936 by a 40hp Fowler 0-4-0 diesel-mechanical works No 21442, painted in green livery. It made its last shunting operation on 29 October 1980 and on closure of the sidings, was transferred to the Swindon & Cricklade Society. Messrs Wills kept the locomotive under cover in the loading bay. Both 620ft long sidings terminated in a warehouse which could be closed by a drop shutter. A semaphore signal provided on the front of the warehouse verandah worked with the shutter and when the shutter was closed, the signal stood at danger, thus offering protection. In 1971 the siding dealt with two to three vans daily.

The Pressed Steel Fisher (PSF) factory was laid out for rail transport with access at both ends of the buildings, raw steel entering on one platform and the finished product emerging at the other. Rail access to the factory opened in 1958. Today five vans are placed in a loading bay — this number being economic to handle and the maximum length for the headshunt between a pair of points and a level crossing gate. A warning bell rings when a train comes into a shipping deck. Safety is important and no loose shunting is permitted. Pressings on pallets loaded by fork lift trucks, have to be carried in covered vans as they are untreated steel and would readily rust. At one time assembled car bodies were despatched, until PSF realised that it was paying for rail vans mostly filled with air! PSF Swindon presses 90% of Metro panels, the majority of which travel by rail.

PSF locomotives have a crew of three: a driver and two shunters — one near the driver and one at the other end of a rake of wagons to protect road crossings in addition to the electrically operated lifting barriers. VAA, VBA and VAB vans

Left: Moredon: main MSWJR line right; power station sidings left. 21 April 1965. *Author*

Right: 0-4-0 Fowler ex-W. D. &. H. O. Wills, Swindon, at Swindon & Cricklade Railway's depot, Blunsdon, 16 August 1982. *Author*

Left: Pressed Steel Fisher: Vans being loaded with pallets of pressings at rail deck, C Building, 4 August 1982. *Author*

are used. The train of 32 vans containing car pressings for Longbridge has to be ready by 15.30-15.45, a PSF locomotive drawing wagons to the BR sidings. Trains are run on only four days a week as a four night week is worked at Longbridge. The BR engine returns from Longbridge with the previous day's empties. In addition to handling wagons of raw material and the finished pressings, three to four rakes of 11 tank wagons of heating oil arrive during the winter months. PSF employs its own fulltime platelayer for maintenance, weeding and minor relaying. Some of the track was relaid in July 1980 in order to carry heavier wagons. This work was carried out by outside contractors mostly during the annual holiday, 60lb/yd being replaced by secondhand BR 100lb/yd rail. Only some lengths were relaid and the remaining lighter track is sinking under the weight of heavier wagons. PSF has a problem — should it go to the expense of relaying the remainder, or change to road transport? An interesting feature of the system is a weighbridge for both road and rail vehicles capable of weighing up to 30 tons.

Top: **Pressed Steel Fisher: fuelling station and No 4 4 August 1982.** *Author*

Top right: **Pressed Steel Fisher: Loco No 5 outside the 'Cathedral' (C building pallet park), 4 August 1982.** *Author*

Above: **30ton road/rail weighbridge, Pressed Steel Fisher, 4 August 1982.** *Author*

Right: **B. Woodworth Esq, Pressed Steel Fisher platelayer outside his cabin holding rail gauge, 4 August 1982.** *Author*

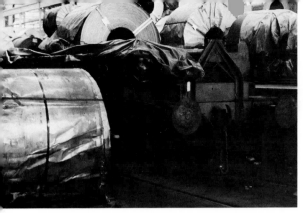

Left: **Pressed Steel Fisher: steel coil in wagon C building. Coil weighs about 15 tons, 4 August 1982.** *Author*

Below: **Pressed Steel Fisher, 4 August 1982. Vans of empty pallets at C building pallet park. Empty vans then moved to C building for loading.** *Author*

Bottom: **'08' Class No 3358 with empty ballast trucks passing under Springfield Road Bridge, after taking ballast to Swindon Town for M4 motorway. 1 May 1971.** *T. G. Flinders*

Until 1982 PSF had six locomotives:

No		Builder	Works No	Date
SBL 1	0-4-0 diesel-mechanical	Fowler	4210105	1955
SBL 2	0-4-0 diesel-mechanical	Fowler	4210137	1958
SBL 3	0-4-0 diesel-hydraulic	Fowler	4220009	1960
SBL 4	0-4-0 diesel-hydraulic	Fowler	4220017	1961
SBL 5	0-4-0 diesel-hydraulic	Fowler	4220018	1961
14	0-4-0 diesel-hydraulic	Fowler	4220032	1965*

*Ex-Cowley Works, Oxford

Nos 1 and 2, the diesel-mechanical locomotives went to the Swindon & Cricklade Railway in July 1982: one engine will be a runner and the other scrapped after spare parts have been removed. Apart from No 14, all the PSF engines are in blue livery lined with white, but No 14, nicknamed 'Cowley Queen' as she came from Cowley circa 1976, is green. The locomotives are cleaned by the drivers and maintained by PSF in Tool Room No 1 which is equipped with pit and battery charger. A flexible pipe is connected to the exhaust when the engine is running inside the building so that the mechanics are not overcome by fumes. Tyres are put on by British Rail Engineering Ltd, the locos travelling to the Works with a BR pilotman. PSF locomotives are normally left outside at night, but in winter are parked in a building to protect them from extreme cold. 100 gallons of diesel fuel are put in the tanks fortnightly. Sand used to be bought from British Rail, but is now purchased from another company, a ton lasting about six months. Today one engine works on day shift and one on the night shift, whereas in 1962 there were four engines running. Because of the presence of nearby dwellings, rail movements have to cease at 23.00 and are not allowed to start until 06.00.

Gorse Hill Gasworks, Swindon was north of the main line and west of Highworth Junction and served by a rail siding. Coal originally came from

Left: **Runaways at Swindon Town, 14 September 1970. Boys had released wagon brakes and trucks ran off end of siding.**
Collection: I. Huddy

Centre left: **No 08.411 passing Swindon station with up transfer goods, 2 June 1982.** *Author*

Below: **Crane No DRA 81553 used for lifting track from Newburn sidings, 2 June 1982.** *Author*

Below right: **PWM No 650 at Swindon, 2 June 1982.** *Author*

Radstock via the Somerset & Dorset Railway to Templecombe, the LSWR to Andover and the SMAR to Swindon Junction and then the GWR. Latterly the sidings were worked by a Ruston & Hornsby diesel-mechanical 0-4-0 works No 418792 of 1959. On closure of the gas works in 1968 it was transferred to Seabank Gasworks, Avonmouth.

In 1970-1 when the M4 Motorway was being built near Swindon, an 800-ton stone train ran from Merehead Quarry near Frome most days and was hauled in three sections by diesel-electric shunter from Rushey Platt to the railhead at Swindon Town.

Until c1979 about three vans a week went to Fyffe's banana depot west of the BR goods shed, also there was an adjacent bulk cement siding from 1979-81 when about a dozen hoppers a week were discharged into a silo. The GWR General Stores was at Swindon and stores vans were sent out with various items such as soap, brushes, towels and polish. Until c1908 the GWR fired bricks at Swindon in a kiln adjacent to the running shed. British Rail's own freight has diminished: the three trains to Swindon Works in 1971 having been reduced to one today. Until lifted in 1982, there were four Civil Engineer's sidings at Newburn, opposite the west end of the Works, used for laying out sections of track. The sidings were worked by Class 08 locomotives from BR stock if departmental PWM 650 was unavailable. Cockleberry Yard between Whitehouse Road bridge and Cricklade Road bridge on the up side is used today for Engineer's vehicles and traffic sidings. At Spike Siding between Cricklade Road and the gas works

opposite the goods shed, the first four roads were for assembling Civil Engineer's trains prior to weekend working and two roads for special load vehicles, for instance where a wooden frame might be fixed for supporting a ship's propeller.

The picture of freight traffic at Swidon today is of a train of Mini Metro panels running from PSF Swindon to Longbridge at 17.40; coils of steel for the pressings coming from South Wales, Scotland and Poole Docks — some by road and some by rail leaving options open in the event of a road or rail strike; Jack Dean (Oils) Ltd in the vee of Highworth Junction has about 10 oil tanks a week, a train from South Wales being divided at Swindon, half going to Jack Dean, Swindon and half to the same firm's siding at Melksham.

In November 1982 a contract started with Anchor brand butter, about five vehicles daily being taken by Freightliner, the wagons detached at Swindon Transfer Yard where the containers are unloaded by crane on hire from Messrs Sparrow. Swindon goods shed, used by National Carriers Ltd for the last 10 years, is in the process of being sold. There is a yard to which a customer can bring traffic, but he has to load and off load rail to road or vice versa himself. The yard has been without a crane since 1980. An example of occasional traffic is a MAN/VW coach chassis which arrived by rail from Germany to be bodied at the MAN/VW depot, Swindon.

Coopers (Metals) Ltd, Gypsy Lane Works, have a yard for chopping scrap metal into furnace size situated on part of the old Swindon Munitions Factory site, west of the Highworth branch. There are two sidings, one of which was relaid in August 1982. A Fowler 0-4-0 diesel-mechanical

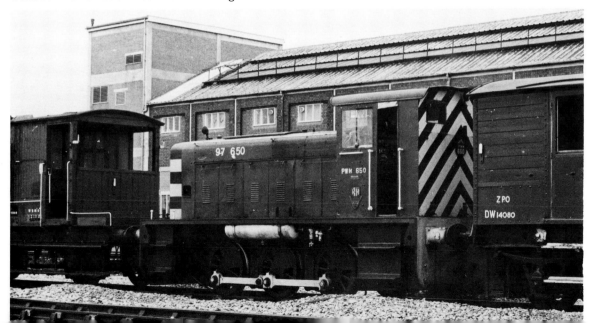

No 4210082 of 1953 ex-Royal Ordnance Factory, Puriton, Somerset, is stabled on one of the sidings, but has not been used. It was the policy of Messrs Cooper to use rail transport whenever possible and c1972 three-quarters of the company's transits were by rail, three trains being turned round daily at its Swindon depot, but owing to British Rail eliminating discounts for small firms, rail transport was made uncompetitive and today hardly any use is made of rail, a little scrap arriving, but scarcely any being despatched. Scrap used to come by rail from the adjacent PSF factory, but now it is collected by road using skips, this method avoiding demurrage on rail wagons. Bremell sidings on the Cheltenham line three miles north of Swindon Junction opened

7 November 1943. Although fuel normally comes by pipe line, petrol is temporarily pumped into rail tankers prior to cleaning the storage tanks.

The MSWJR provided an excellent service — goods collected in London in the afternoon being ready for delivery in Swindon early next morning. In 1958 three fitted freights running each way between Cheltenham and Andover were withdrawn leaving only local goods services south of Cirencester and nothing north of the town. When most of the line closed on 9 September 1961 the line was still kept open from Rushey Platt to Swindon Town and Cirencester. From 19 May 1964 Swindon Town handled only coal traffic and oil tanks for Esso, and from 1 November 1966 Esso oil tanks only on a private siding basis.

Left: **No D1020** *Western Hero* **heads an up freight through Swindon, 11 June 1963.** *A. Swain*

Below left: **Class 47 No 47.237 at the head of an empty hoppers train bound for South Wales, 5 November 1975.** *Brian Morrison*

Below: **VW/MAN chassis on Belgian wagon at Swindon, 2 June 1982.** *Author*

Bottom: **Re-ballasting siding, Coopers (Metals) Ltd, Swindon, 4 August 1982.** *Author*

The Great Western Railway Works & the Locomotive Power Scene

When the line from London to Bristol was nearing completion, the need arose for a central repair depot for the locomotives so Daniel Gooch was asked to investigate and report on the best location. On 13 September 1840 he wrote a letter to Brunel using these arguments in favour of Swindon:

a) It was the junction with the Cheltenham line.
b) East of Swindon the line was virtually flat, whereas to the west were the 1 in 100 gradients of Wootton Bassett and Box and bank engines for the former incline could be shedded at Swindon.
c) The selection of Swindon would divide the line into three equal parts: to Reading; to Swindon and to Bristol.
d) The railway crossed the Wilts & Berks Canal at Swindon giving a direct connection with the Somerset coalfield. (It is interesting that locomotive coal came by water). The canal and its reservoir at Coate could supply water in an emergency.

On 25 February 1841 the directors concurred with Gooch, their minute book reading: 'Decide to provide an engine establishment at Swindon commensurate with the wants of the Company, where a change of engines may be advantageously made and the trains stopped for the purpose of passengers taking refreshment ... The establishment there would also comprehend the large repairing shops for the Locomotive Department; and this circumstance rendered it necessary to arrange for the building of Cottages, etc, for the residence of many persons employed in the service of the Company'.

The erection of workshops for the repair of locomotives was commenced without delay, notice that only 'repair' is mentioned; it is doubtful if new construction was considered at this stage. The Works was built on land belonging to the Cheltenham & Great Western Union Railway providing 'that arrangements for all requisite accommodation, both at the engine house and the passenger station, were made for working the Cheltenham line separately'. The stone used for constructing the Works was obtained from cutting Box Tunnel. The Works buildings have arches in the walls, most of which are bricked up, the object of the design being so that if a new door was required, stones could be knocked out without the wall collapsing. The present Radiator Shop is an 18th century barn of the farm on which the Works was built. Double glazing was installed in the 1840s to keep some of the sound out of the office buildings.

The machinery was started in November 1842, but the works was not in regular operation until 2 January 1843 and on this date, over 423 men were employed, 72 being highly skilled engineers. The first works manager was Archibald Sturrock, later locomotive superintendent to the Great Northern Railway, Sturrock using many GWR features such as sandwich frames and domeless boilers. Brunel and Gooch were convinced that they could build engines cheaper than outside contractors and the first Swindon built locomotive, the 2-2-2 *Great Western* left the Works in April 1846 only 13 weeks after the date of the order. To complete construction, work proceeded night and day. On 13 June with a train of 100 tons behind the tender, *Great Western* ran from Paddington to Swindon in 78 minutes, this giving an average speed of 60mile/h. The first engine built at Swindon was the 0-6-0 *Premier* completed in February 1846, but as the boiler was not manufactured in the town, it cannot count as the first Swindon engine. Swindon constructed its first standard gauge engine in 1855 and transported it to Wolverhampton on a broad gauge wagon. By September 1849 the Works buildings had doubled in size to cover $14\frac{1}{2}$ acres and had

Right: **Bird's eye view of New Swindon c1850. Works left, St Mark's Church centre, railway village right, station in distance.** *BR*

Below: **Works 1846.**

Bottom: **Works 1901.**

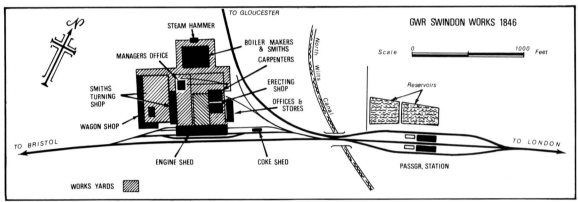

GWR SWINDON WORKS 1846

TO GLOUCESTER

STEAM HAMMER

MANAGERS OFFICE

BOILER MAKERS & SMITHS

CARPENTERS

ERECTING SHOP

OFFICES & STORES

SMITHS TURNING SHOP

WAGON SHOP

North Wilts Canal

Scale 0 — 1000 Feet

Reservoirs

TO BRISTOL

ENGINE SHED

COKE SHED

TO LONDON

PASSGR. STATION

WORKS YARDS

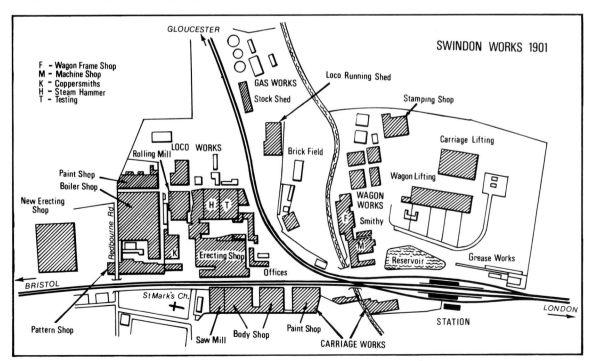

SWINDON WORKS 1901

GLOUCESTER

F – Wagon Frame Shop
M – Machine Shop
K – Coppersmiths
H – Steam Hammer
T – Testing

GAS WORKS

Stock Shed

Loco Running Shed

Stamping Shop

Carriage Lifting

LOCO WORKS

Rolling Mill

Brick Field

Wagon Lifting

Paint Shop

Boiler Shop

New Erecting Shop

Redbourne Rd

H T

Erecting Shop

K

WAGON WORKS

F Smithy

M

Reservoir

Grease Works

Offices

BRISTOL

St Mark's Ch.

Pattern Shop

Saw Mill

Body Shop

Paint Shop

CARRIAGE WORKS

STATION

LONDON

39

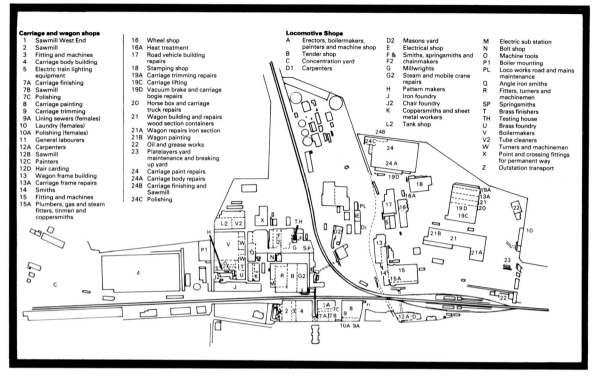

Carriage and wagon shops

1 Sawmill West End
2 Sawmill
3 Fitting and machines
4 Carriage body building
5 Electric train lighting equipment
7A Carriage finishing
7B Sawmill
7C Polishing
8 Carriage painting
9 Carriage trimming
9A Lining sewers (females)
10 Laundry (females)
10A Polishing (females)
11 General labourers
12A Carpenters
12B Sawmill
12C Painters
12D Hair carding
13 Wagon frame building
13A Carriage frame repairs
14 Smiths
15 Fitting and machines
15A Plumbers, gas and steam fitters, tinmen and coppersmiths

16 Wheel shop
16A Heat treatment
17 Road vehicle building repairs
18 Stamping shop
19A Carriage trimming repairs
19C Carriage lifting
19D Vacuum brake and carriage bogie repairs
20 Horse box and carriage truck repairs
21 Wagon building and repairs wood section containers
21A Wagon repairs iron section
21B Wagon painting
22 Oil and grease works
23 Platelayers yard maintenance and breaking up yard
24 Carriage paint repairs
24A Carriage body repairs
24B Carriage finishing and Sawmill
24C Polishing

Locomotive Shops

A Erectors, boilermakers, painters and machine shop
B Tender shop
C Concentration yard
D1 Carpenters
D2 Masons yard
E Electrical shop
F & Smiths, springsmiths and chainmakers
G Millwrights
G2 Steam and mobile crane repairs
H Pattern makers
J Iron foundry
J2 Chair foundry
K Coppersmiths and sheet metal workers
L2 Tank shop

M Electric sub station
N Bolt shop
O Machine tools
P1 Boiler mounting
PL Loco works road and mains maintenance
Q Angle iron smiths
R Fitters, turners and machinemen
SP Springsmiths
T Brass finishers
TH Testing house
U Brass foundry
V Boilermakers
V2 Tube cleaners
W Turners and machinemen
X Point and crossing fittings for permanent way
Z Outstation transport

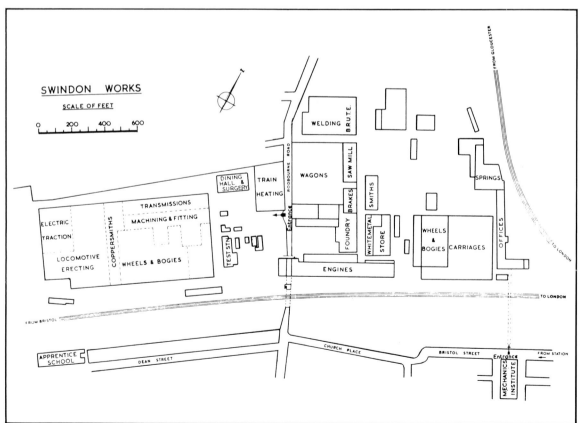

SWINDON WORKS

SCALE OF FEET

0   200   400   600

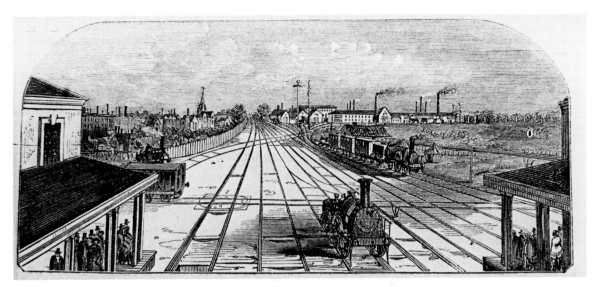

Above: **Swindon Junction c1850, view to Works from station footbridge.** *George Measom*

Left: **Works 1954.**

Below left: **Works 1971.**

started to diversify, as that year the Isis bridge for the Oxford & Rugby line was built at Swindon. In 1861 a rail mill was built capable of producing 19,300 tons of rail annually, but closed in the 1870s when steel rails came into use and it was found that outside contractors could produce rails more cheaply. The carriage works were transferred to Swindon in June 1868. In 1921 the Carriage & Wagon Works were in two portions: one sited on the south of the main line to Bristol which dealt with nothing but woodwork, the coaches travelling progressively eastwards as various stages were completed. All steel and iron work was made in the new extensions to the wagon works which lay north of the railway behind the station. In these latter works, in addition to providing the metal work for coaches, all wagons were built and repaired, repairs to coaches being transferred from the old carriage works. There were also miscellaneous shops for the manufacture of road motors, carts, vans and so on. Many of the GWR road wagon builders received their initial training in the small yards in the surrounding towns and villages, a road wagon builder, like a carriage builder, having to be a craftsman. An economical adjunct to the new sawmills was the sawdust gas producer plant

used to supply gas for the engines which drove machinery for lighting the mill. The four cylinder engine having an output of 320bhp at 220rpm was directly coupled to a dc generator with a capacity of 220kW at 250v. All sawdust, shavings and bits of wood from the mill were used.

New foundries were built in 1873 and two years later the workforce totalled 4,000, a further 500 coming on the books in 1876. In 1888 the gas works was extended and automatic stoking machinery installed. At the time it was the largest gas plant in Europe and supplied gas to the housing estate as well as the Works. Due economy was realised by discontinuing street lighting on the three nights either side of a full moon. The gasworks closed about 1959.

To cope with the problem of broad gauge stock at final conversion, in 1891 sidings were constructed at a cost of £8,500 on 10 acres at a site immediately west of Rodbourne Road, 13 miles of sidings being laid. Conversion of rolling stock cost £374,000. A bogie coach was changed from broad to standard gauge as a special effort in 10 minutes before a party of directors, but could easily be done normally in 20 minutes, the operation merely a matter of changing the bogies and altering the footboards; on one occasion 25 coaches were converted in $6\frac{1}{4}$ hours by means of specially constructed hydraulic trap lifts. T. I. Allen, assistant manager of the GWR said, 'We had a party of directors from one of the northern lines down at Swindon recently, travelling in saloons on the broad gauge. While they were looking at the Works, the bodies of the carriages were lifted on to narrow gauge frames, and they were sent on without changing their carriages from the Great

Right: **Trimming shop, Swindon Works.** *Swindon Reference Library*

Left: **French polishing shop.** *Swindon Reference Library*

Below: **Carriage body erecting shop, Swindon Works c1920.** *GWR Magazine*

Right: **Foundry.**
Swindon Reference Library

Left: **Producer plant, sawmills.**
Swindon Reference Library

Below: **WR locos withdrawn from service stored at BR Swindon gas works, 22 November 1959.**
W. Potter

Below: Gas tank wagons at Swindon BR gas works, August 1965. *D. J. Hyde*

Bottom: Diesel railcar No W21W at Swindon BR gas works. *D. J. Hyde*

Right: Swindon scrapyard 1892, broad gauge engines. *LPC*

Western line, to, I think, the Midland, at Gloucester'. For many years the GWR had built convertible engines and the gauge of these was altered relatively simply. In fact, of the 195 broad gauge locomotives in stock in May 1892, 130 were convertible. There were 748 coaching stock vehicles and over 3,400 wagons and vans.

When the broad gauge was converted, extra men were taken on at the Works, every village and hamlet for miles around sending its unemployed. Men were engaged in cutting down or breaking up coaches, wagons and engines, little skill being necessary for the last two. Wages at the Works, although comparatively low, were much higher than those of a farm labourer. Within a radius of six to 10 miles of Swindon, only the feeble and decrepit worked on farms, those who failed the physical tests, or those who had worked at the factory but discharged through old age or other unfitness.

In 1892 it was claimed that the Works was 'the largest establishment in the world for the manufacture and repair of railway engines, carriages and wagons, almost 10,000 men being employed under one management. The Works produced one new engine a week, one new coach every day and one new wagon every working hour. Distribution of staff was:

Locomotive Department

Locomotive factory	5,000	
Rolling mills	300	
Running shed	300	5,600

Carriage Department

Carriage works	1,800	
Saw mill	400	2,200
Wagon works		1,600
Office staff		300
Railway owned stores, platelayers' dept, etc		350
		10,050

A laundry was opened in November 1892 for washing railway owned articles arriving in baskets from all over the GWR system. In 1930 towels were the most common item washed, providing 2,800,000 out of the 3,000,000 annual articles, the laundry using each year a total of 10 tons of

Left: **View of 'A' shop, 15 August 1954.** *W. Potter*

Below: **'A' shop c1910.** *Swindon Reference Library*

Bottom: **Swindon 'A' shop No 6813** *Eastbury Grange* **and No 3671, 1 December 1963.** *Hugh Ballantyne*

Left: **Aerial view of Swindon c1912.** *Courtesy Pendon Museum*

Below left: **View of Works from top of Hambro Life building. 2 June 1982.** *Author*

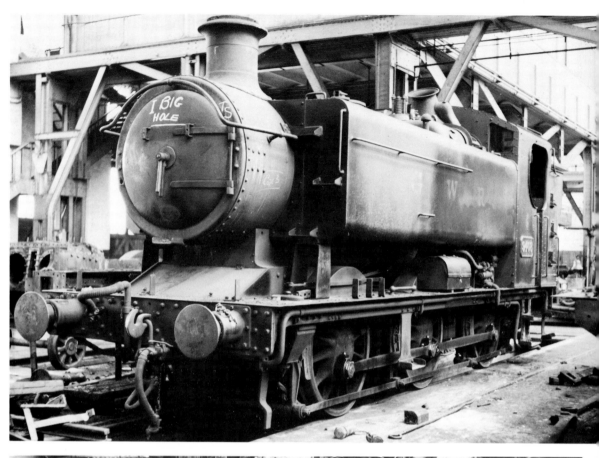

Above: No 6001 *King Edward VII* on test plant c1954. BR

Left: Vale of Rheidol 2-6-2T No 8 being reassembled at Swindon after major overhaul, 26 May 1954. *Hugh Ballantyne*

Below: 'A' wheel shop. *Courtesy Pendon Museum*

Above left: No 9408, still lettered GWR, undergoing repair, 24 February 1957. *Hugh Ballantyne*

Left: 'A' shop and *North Star*. 6 March 1955. *W. Potter*

Left: **Machine and turning shop No 2.** *Swindon Reference Library*

Below left: **LMS No 8469 designed by W. A. Stanier, built at Swindon by GWR. Running on GWR iron ore train at Bishop's Cleeve, April 1945, having emerged new from the Works only the previous month.** *W. Potter*

Below: **No 92220** *Evening Star* **inside 'A' shop shortly after the naming ceremony 18 March 1960.** *Hugh Ballantyne*

Below right: **As part of the** *Evening Star* **naming celebrations, Caledonian Railway No 123 was displayed in 'A' shop, 18 March 1960.** *Hugh Ballantyne*

Great Western prepared soap powder. The GWR had a grease and soap works also in Whitehouse Road. The former GWR laundry is now used as a hospital laundry. Between 1901 and 1903 Erecting Shop 'A' was opened. Covering $5\frac{3}{4}$ acres and built on the site of the broad gauge sidings laid in 1891, it was described by G. A. Sekon in the *Railway Magazine* for October 1901. 'Its vastness appals one . . . Mere figures convey no idea of its size to the ordinary mind; within this shop could be comfortably accommodated two parallel streets of lower middle-class villas, each street of the modern regulation width of 40ft, with four rows of 30 houses each, with the usual forecourts and back gardens. Now you have it — a roof big enough to cover 120 suburban residences, gardens, road and all!' In 1919 the shop was almost doubled in size to cover $11\frac{1}{2}$ acres, which at the time of building made it the largest permanent workshop in Europe. An interesting feature is the fact that the offices and toilets are situated in the roof to make maximum use of the floor space. One interesting feature of the Works was that locomotive boilers were sent under Rodbourne Road from the Boiler Shop to the Boiler Testing Shop.

During World War 1 the Works turned out various heavy howitzers and 60 pounder Hotchkiss and AA guns; large quantities of medium and heavy calibre shells, bombs, mines and parts for submarines and paravanes. A large quantity of toluol was also produced for use in the manufacture of TNT explosive. Dean goods 0-6-0s were converted for War Department use in France and the Middle East and 16 ambulance trains each of 15 coaches were prepared from existing stock. All this was in addition to the everyday work of the factory.

In 1935, the Centenary year, over 1,000 locomotives were repaired and the Works had a capacity for building two new engines a week, the annual capacity of the carriage works was 250 passenger vehicles of various types and repair of 5,000; 3,000 of these being in the nature of heavy repairs. The wagon works was capable of constructing 4,500 new wagons and of repairing about 8,000. In 1938 the 1,800ft long Carriage Stock Shed paid for by a Government loan, was completed. It was built on the south side of the Bristol line on the site of Newbury House, home of the GWR CMEs. It stored on 10 roads 265 coaches when these were not required for summer services.

In World War 2 the Works assisted in building gun mountings, turret rings for armoured cars, pom pom guns, the first 2,000 and 4,000lb bombs more than 2,000 of the latter being turned out, armour plating for AFVs (armoured fighting vehicles), timber components for Bailey bridges, Short Stirling bombers, 50 midget submarine superstructures, and artificial limbs. The wagon shop built a large number of motor landing craft. The GWR also provided ambulance trains. USA servicemen who lived in coaches outside No 19

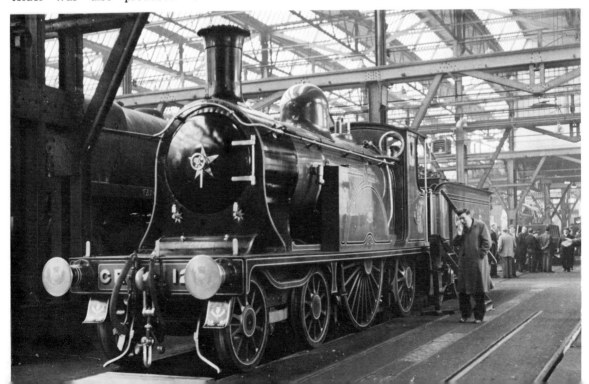

Above: Railcar No 4 restored to GWR livery and on display 18 March 1960. *Hugh Ballantyne*

Left: Broad gauge driving wheels from Bristol & Exeter 4-2-4T at Swindon Works 18 August 1957. *W. Potter*

Below left: Iron Mink F van outside the General Stores. Two of these vans were used as additional store accommodation for a number of years, only moving occasionally inside the Works. Originally they were used for general goods and parcels work between Paddington and Bristol and lettered thus. August 1965. *D. J. Hyde*

Above right: WR steam roller No 7 on bogie wagon No 40994, Swindon Works, 5 May 1957. *W. Potter*

Carriage Lifting Shop were employed in various shops converting stock into ambulance trains. American locomotives were received in the AE shop. Dean Goods locomotives were again converted for war service and LMS Stanier 2-8-0 locomotives Nos 8400-79 produced for use in the United Kingdom. They outlived the GWR 2-8-0s, No 48476 being one of the locomotives used on the Railway Correspondence & Travel Society's last steam hauled special 4 August 1968.

At Nationalisation in 1948 the Works covered 326 acres, 77½ of which were roofed. At this time the majority of the machinery was electrically driven, absorbing approximately a quarter of the output from Moredon power station. With the retirement of Frederick William Hawksworth as CME of the Western Region in 1949, unified control at Swindon terminated; the Locomotive Works, Running Department and Carriage & Wagon Department each being placed under separate authority.

Class D800 'Warship' class diesel-hydraulic engines were built at Swindon in 1957 and in 1959 a new Points & Crossings Shop was opened bringing the roofed area up to about 85 acres. The last steam locomotive built for BR, No 92220 *Evening Star* was turned out from Swindon on 18 March 1960, the last GWR type steam engine built at Swindon being 0-6-0PT No 1669 in May 1955. In the late 1950s and early 1960s Swindon was turning out diesel-mechanical shunters, diesel-hydraulic 'D8xx' and 'D10xx' class loco-

motives as well as Inter-City the Cross Country DMUs.

The 'Main Workshops Future Plan' of 1962 called for the closure of 15 of the 31 BR works in the country. At Swindon the Carriage & Wagon Works closed in 1967 and the site sold to Swindon Borough Council, coaching stock having ceased to be built at Swindon in 1962, new carriage construction being concentrated at Derby and York. The locomotive works was modified to undertake repair of carriages and wagons in addition to locomotives. This was done at a cost of £2.3million out of the £17million made available by the government. The staff was reduced during this period from 9,000 to 6,000. The 1962 Plan meant that all BR works were transferred to a central authority, being reorganised and rationalised on a national basis, the workload being considered from a total, instead of a regional angle. Under the 1968 Transport Act, the central workshops authority was turned into a limited company, wholly owned by BRB, but self-accounting. The Act gave BREL the right, when it had spare capacity, to accept outside tenders, some of the earliest at Swindon being deck hatches for cargo ships, reconditioning engines for marine research vessels and air-intake splitter housings for large gas turbines. Many bus operators have been pleased to make use of the facilities offered to keep their fleets in operation, not only for engine work, but also for repairs and modifications to the bodies and upholstery, the Works dealing with

nearly 200 single-deck buses for the Bristol Omnibus Company in 1973. Road passenger transport vehicles were not unusual to Swindon men as we have seen that the GWR had its own Vehicle Body Workshops for motor and horse drawn vehicles and it removed and repaired Swindon Corporation electric tramcar No 11 after its overturn at Regent's Circus on 1 June 1906, the brakes being modified by the GWR's C. B. Collett. All available members of the fleet of 13 double-deck, open top, electric trams were used at lunch and tea times, at least four cars waiting at the Works exits in Rodbourne Road and another five or six in Faringdon Road at its nearest point to the Tunnel entrance, the remaining cars being at the depot for servicing or repairs. In 1974 the Works built 42 bodies for export coaches under an order placed by the Gloucester Railway Carriage & Wagon Co Ltd. The gradual withdrawal of the diesel-hydraulic locomotives in the early 1970s resulted in a further reduction of the workforce, 1,262 jobs going in 1972-3 and by 1975 the Works occupied an area of 147 acres of which 34 were

roofed. In 1982 the freehold value of BREL land at Swindon was £100,000 an acre.

In 1979 Swindon built its first locomotive for 14 years and its first ever export locomotive, the Works providing 20 of the 36 shunters ordered by Kenyan Railways from Hunslet. They were metre gauge 0-8-0 525hp diesel-hydraulic engines, very similar to the 'Teddy Bear' Class 14 650hp 0-6-0 shunter, No D9555 of which was the last previous new locomotive to leave Swindon Works in October 1965. A metre gauge test track was built and if an engine could negotiate a kink in the layout without being derailed, it was deemed satisfactory. Since 1846 approximately 6,000 locomotives have been constructed at Swindon. In 1982 DMUs and '08' shunters were repaired and Class 411 EMUS refurbished. The practice of handpainting has been reverted to as it was found that weather penetrated spray-painted coaches. Gardner marine engines are repaired, today the Works being the only firm to carry out this task. Tinsmiths at Swindon make tail lamps for the whole of BR. The present brake equipment repair

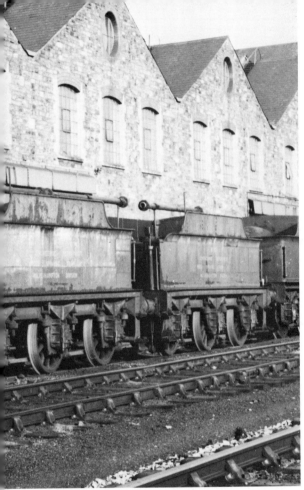

Left: **WR Engineering Department Weed Killing train No 2, Wolverhampton Division, at Swindon Works 27 January 1957.** *W. Potter*

Above: **Drinking water tank at Swindon Works, 14 August 1955.** *W. Potter*

Below: **Road wagon shop.** *Swindon Reference Library*

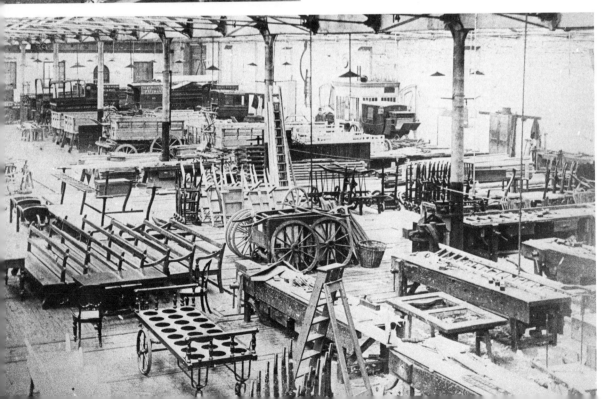

Left: **Metre/standard gauge traversing table, Swindon Works, 24 August 1982.** *Author*

Below left: **Curve at Swindon Works to test metre gauge locos, 24 August 1982.** *Author*

Right: **No 11 Brake Equipment Repair Shop. This was originally the broad gauge loco shop and the doorway is tall enough for the chimney of a broad gauge engine. 24 August 1982.** *Author*

Below: **Swindon Works from the south east, 2 June 1982.** *Author*

Above: Refurbished DMU outside Swindon Works, 2 June 1982. *Author*

Left: Tyring pit, Swindon Works, to heat tyre to expand over wheel centre, 24 August 1982.   *Author*

Below: Reprofiling wheels of No 34081 *92 Squadron* from the Nene Valley Railway, 24 August 1982. *Author*

Above left: Bogie store, Swindon Works, 24 August 1982.   *Author*

Left: Water tower, Swindon Works. Wooden patterns are stored in the building below the tanks. 2 June 1982.   *Author*

shop was the original broad gauge locomotive shop and has an extra tall arch for the broad gauge engine which had a higher loading gauge than the 'Kings'.

Calibrations are done for other BREL works, Swindon providing masters to National Physical Laboratory standards. Coil springs were made and leaf springs repaired. When leaf springs were made at Swindon, there was a saying that 'The bloke on the hammer makes the difference between the tea staying in the cup, or going in the saucer'. On a very hot day, the temperature in the furnace area can rise to 142°F, with men drinking up to two gallons of real barley water a day supplied by BREL. In the Chain Shop chains and ropes are made up. Swindon has one of the oldest chain testing houses in the country, a machine built in 1874 still being used. Tests are done for anyone — British Leyland, the Water Board, Southern Electricity, British Telecom — all lifting gear having a 100% overload test. British Rail Universal Trolley Equipment (BRUTE) trolleys were manufactured for all BR regions and for supply to outside undertakings. The Works boasts of the only non-ferrous metal foundry within BREL. The aluminium coach doors when first cast in one piece were the largest castings made anywhere in the world in that metal less than 5mm thick.

All the shops have sparrows living in them. As they have lived there for about 130 years, they have become modified. Compared with a standard sparrow, the Swindon sparrow has two flight feathers missing on each wing and has yellow feathers around its throat. They are fed by the men and never go out. Workmen go in during the holidays to feed them and also the cats. Rabbits are also to be found within the Works, some having rust in their intestines due to the rusty land on which they graze. At one time Irishmen cleaning out boiler tubes and sleeping in old coaches caught the rabbits for making into stew.

When the Works first opened, the hours were 6am to 6pm, which with meal breaks gave a

Below: **Stage 1 of rebuilding an EMU, Swindon Works, 24 August 1982.** *Author*

Right: **Refurbishing DMUs, 24 August 1982.** *Author*

Below right: **Restaurant car being converted into a Camping Coach, 'A' shop, 24 August 1982.** *Author*

57½hr week. In 1866 one hour less was worked on Saturdays. A 9hr day was introduced in 1872 making a 54hr week, which in 1919 became a 47hr week. Today the 3,500 men work a 39hr week 7.30am-12.30pm; 1.15-4.30pm and a finishing time of 1.30pm on Friday. Four minutes are allowed for clocking in at the shop where they are employed. Formerly thousands of bicycles were used and some people whose gardens were near the Works entrance stored machines for a certain sum per week, receiving a worthwhile supplementary income when one realises whole gardens were filled. The Works has more first aid boxes than most factories, an above average number of workers being trained St John's Ambulancemen and all apprentices taught first aid. Until about 15 years ago, Wiltshire used the Works fire brigade for fire fighting in the town, the Works supplying two crews. Part time firemen, they normally worked in the factory. Fire engines proved useful on 1 February 1911 when the night watchman saw flames in the carriage paint shop. Works and Borough brigades were on the scene quickly and the Royal coach was just drawn out in time. The shop could not be saved, so the Works engine at one end and the Borough engine at the other, used their efforts to prevent the fire spread-

Above left: **No 08.696, 24 August 1982.** *Author*

Left: **Base plates, permanent way depot, Swindon, 16 August 1982.** *Author*

Above: **Nos 03.062 and ADB975773 — Swindon R&M (Running & Maintenance) Breakdown Unit, 16 August 1982.** *Author*

Right: **Tunnel entrance to the Works, 16 August 1982.** *Author*

ing to adjoining shops. The 137 men in the paint shop were thrown temporarily out of work. The fire station is situated by the former carriage works adjacent to No 2 Saw Mill — near the site where the greatest fire risk was. Firemen's houses in the railway village were connected to the fire station by an electric alarm.

For an annual sum of £300 the canal company provided the Works with water from Coate reservoir, though in the latter half of the last century most of the water for the Works and running shed was obtained by operating water trains of old tenders from Kemble to Swindon. In 1885 a 736ft deep well was sunk in the Works,

Left: GWR workers returning home in the evening c1920.
Swindon Reference Library

Right: Pay table, Swindon Works, 24 August 1982.   *Author*

Left: 1942 Dennis fire engine, in BR Fire Station, Swindon, formerly the GWR school. 16 August 1982. *Author*

Right: Alarm buttons in BR fire station, formerly used to alert firemen in railwaymen's cottages, 16 August 1982. *Author*

Below: Original pumphouse to pump water from North Wilts Canal to Works, 16 August 1982. *Author*

Above: **Hooters above Hooter House, 24 August 1982.** *Author*

Below: **Hooter timetable 24 August 1982.** *Author*

SWINDON WORKS HOOTER				
	MONDAY to THURSDAY		FRIDAY	
	TIME	DURATION	TIME	DURATION
M O R N I N G	6·45	17 SECS	6·45	17 SECS
	7·20	12 SECS	7·20	12 SECS
	7·25	7 SECS	7·25	7 SECS
	7·30	12 SECS	7·30	12 SECS
	12·30	12 SECS	1·30	12 SECS
A F T E R N O O N	1·05	12 SECS		
	1·10	7 SECS		
	1·15	12 SECS		
	4·30	12 SECS		

but was found to contain five times the normal quantity of salt and was therefore useless. By 1903 the Works required more water than the canal and tenders could provide, so new wells and a steam pumping plant were put into operation on the down platform at Kemble 12½ miles distant on the Cheltenham line, the work being finished in December 1903 and the pipeline to Swindon opened. Although since 1935 the pumps have been electrically powered, until the end of steam locomotives, a Swindon Works trial engine ran to Kemble on the first Thursday of every month in order to run the pumps for a short period to keep the steam operated standby pumps in working condition, should they need to be used in the event of an electrical failure, in which event a Pannier tank was sent to Kemble under class 'A' headlamps and steam obtained from its injector steam valves. Prior to the installation of the electric pumps, this procedure also took place when the boiler at Kemble was due for maintenance. In the event of the 'Burst Pipe' indicator operating at Kemble signalbox, if the fall of pressure was due to a real burst and not just a pump failure, a light engine was required to propel a shunting truck fitted with a lighting set over the down main line from Swindon Loco Yard to Kemble to check if water escaping from the burst had damaged the track. If the down line was unsafe, but the up intact, then single line working was instituted. Today in the event of a burst a 'light diesel' would be sent to Kemble to investigate the condition of the track. If damaged, the road would be closed and trains diverted, a bus service operating to and from Kemble.

The loud Works hooter is one of the special features of the factory. Men walked in from a distance of nine miles or more and in the last century when personal and domestic timepieces were beyond the pocket of many, a warning was necessary. A large bell was used at first, but steam hooter had come into use by 1867, loud enough to be heard at Highworth and Cricklade six miles away and blown for 10 minutes at 5.20am, three minutes at 5.50am and one minute at 6.00am. In 1872 Lord Bolingbroke complained that it woke him prematurely from his seat at Lydiard Park 3½ miles to the north-west of the Works. The Local Government Board at first came down on the side of the GWR but then revoked sanction for the hooter and it was only through the ingenuity of the Hon F. W. Cadogan, at that time MP for the Cricklade Division, which included Swindon, that a solution was found. Another hooter was fixed on the roof within a few yards of the disused one, and, as the Hon F. W. Cadogan pointed out, although the original hooter might not be blown, no injunction had been granted against the second one, which, incidentally, was louder than the first. The beauty of this process was that it could be repeated indefinitely, a fact apparently recognised by the authorities, for the matter was allowed to drop. A writer in 1935 said that the hooter had been heard at Bourton on the Water 25 miles distant. In the 1960s when it was no longer a requirement for workers to be woken, people complained and the hooters were lowered 30ft. The present hooters are ships' sirens.

Until lifted in 1977, there were sidings between 'A' shop and the MSWJR embankment known colloquially as 'The Dump' and officially as the Factory Pool. Probably laid down during World War 1, they were used for storing locomotives and rolling stock, usually prior to scrapping, but after the Grouping in 1923, some of the engines the GWR had acquired were sent there to await detailed examination. Coaches were on the three roads nearest the main line and locomotives on the other 15 roads. Immediately north of The Dump were two sidings where locomotives were scrapped, about five engines being broken up each fortnight. As the system of breaking up engines in the open was unable to cope with the numerous withdrawals, a cutting-up workshop was erected in 1932 at the north-west corner of The Dump. Unaffected by the weather, cutting up under cover was more rapid, the number of engines on the sidings diminished and the roads were only used for storing locomotives on the Sales List and principally used for storing wagons. On the far north of The Dump was the Saw Mill where whole trees were cut up on large band saws, the timber being stacked in adjacent drying sheds. Today, ashes from the site of The Dump are being sold as a valuable asset as coal can be extracted from the ash. The present day equivalent of The Dump is the Con Yard.

Below: **Cutting up No 5423 in 'C' shop.** *W. Potter*

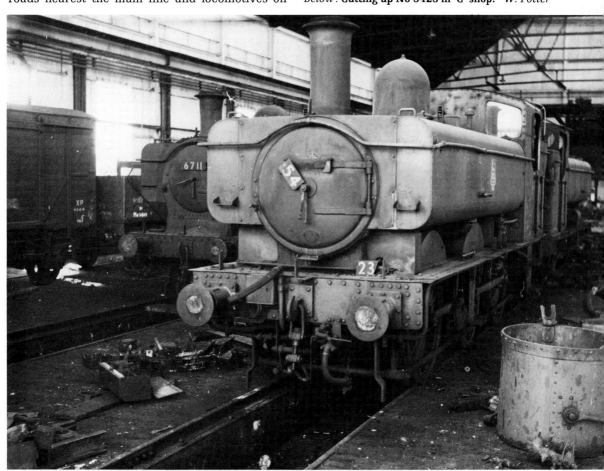

Above: 'V2s' for scrap at Swindon near 'C' shop, (lt-rt) Nos 43112, 60887, 60892, 60894, 60922, 7929 *Wyke Hall*, 60812. 20 September 1964. *Hugh Ballantyne*

Left: Swindon Dump 24 June 1951, (lt-rt) Nos 2947 *Madresfield Court*, 4058 *Princess Augusta*, 1925, 3447 *Jackdaw*, 3451 *Pelican*, 4018 *Knight of the Grand Cross*. *W. Potter*

Left: **Longmoor Military Railway No 8182 ex-Shropshire & Montgomeryshire Railway, LNWR 0-6-0 4ft 3in coal engine awaiting cutting up on the Dump, 24 September 1950.** *W. Potter*

Above: **Works yard 28 March 1954.** *W. Potter*

Left: **Saw mills, c1920.** *GWR Magazine*

The Motive Power Scene

Swindon having the main locomotive works of the GWR, engines of all standard classes would have been seen there. The first broad gauge passenger trains tended to be worked by engines of the 2-2-2 wheel arrangement, while freight was hauled by those of the 0-6-0 variety. Later broad gauge expresses were headed by 4-2-2 engines. Apart from one train each way, in the 1880s, all London to Bristol passenger trains were worked by Westbourne Park 8ft Singles, and by the end of 1880 when 23 were at work, most had been completely renewed. In the 1880s, three 'Hawthorn' class broad gauge 2-4-0s *Acheron*, *Phlegethon* and *Hawk* were stationed at Swindon as pilots. Built 1865-6 they were the last broad gauge coupled tender engines to be built other than the 'Convertibles'. Two of the three stood pilot on alternate days, the third being a spare engine. Because of the excellent maintenance of the express engines, their assistance was rarely required. From about the end of 1885, to avoid

piloting the heavy 3.00pm up express from Bristol, the 4-2-2 which worked the 5.30am newspaper train to Bristol and the 3.00pm up express, was removed at Swindon and replaced by the pilot, though in the event, another engine often had to assist the 'Hawthorn' on the 3.00pm up from Bristol. Two experimental four inside cylinder tandem locomotives appeared in 1886, No 7 being standard gauge and No 8 a broad gauge convertible. No 7 was an indifferent runner and employed on slow trains between Swindon and Cardiff, while No 8 was a failure, both were 'renewed' as 'Armstrong' class 4-4-0s. Convertible 2-4-0s Nos 14 and 16 built at Swindon in 1888, replaced the 'Hawthorn' 2-4-0s as pilots at

Below: **Broad gauge** *Lord of the Isles* **in front of St Mark's Church, Swindon.**
Swindon Reference Library

Above: **No 3440** *City of Truro* **on turntable at the Works, 18 August 1957.** *W. Potter*

Above right: **No 4061** *Glastonbury Abbey* **in Swindon Works with Stephenson Locomotive Society special from Birmingham, 11 September 1955.** *W. Potter*

Right: **GWR steam railcar No 75 at the Works, 27 May 1925.** *GWR*

Swindon also taking over the job of hauling the heavy 3.00pm up express from Bristol to Swindon. They were not directly converted to standard gauge engines, but 'renewed' as 4-4-0s of the 'Armstrong' class in 1894. The last broad gauge engines built at Swindon were the 4-2-2s *Great Western*, *Prometheus* and *Tornado* in 1888 and had a life of less than four years. The last Convertible engine which left Swindon Works was 2-2-2 No 3030 of the '3021' class in December 1891, working for only five months on the broad gauge.

'Sir Daniel' class 2-2-2s shedded at Bristol, worked the standard gauge up express from Bristol to London in the 1880s. By the turn of the century loads had become too heavy for them and they were converted to 0-6-0s for a further lease of life, though looking rather strange in their new guise, the curved framing above the centre wheel being retained. In the 1880s Swindon-based

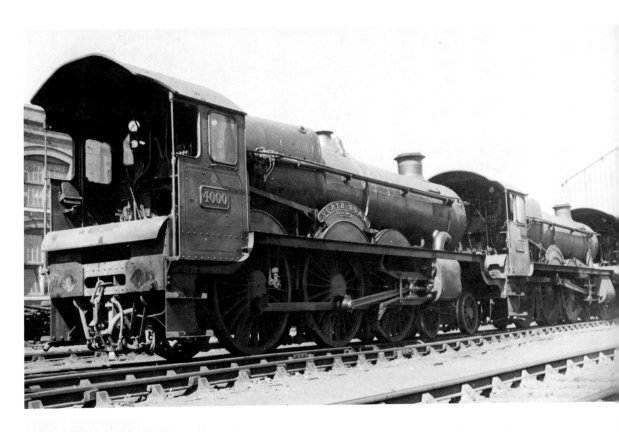

Above left: **No 4000** *North Star* **and No 5913** *Rushton Hall* **on condemned road April 1957.** *Rev A. Newman*

Left: **No 9705, condensing 0-6-0PT, 5 November 1961.** *Hugh Ballantyne*

Top: **No 4410 awaiting Works entry 11 September 1955.** *Hugh Ballantyne*

Above: **No 3015 and No 4551, 19 March 1956. No 3015 has a 'Not to be Moved' disc.** *Rev A. Newman*

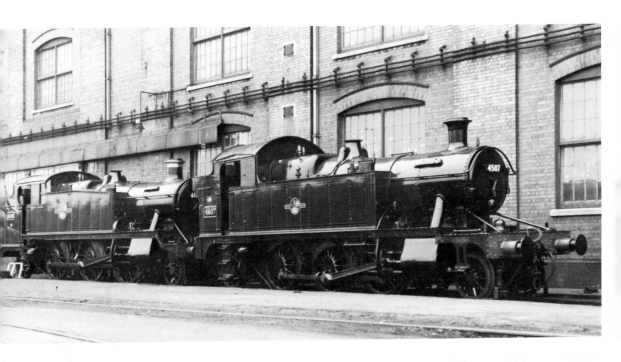

Top: **Nos 4507 and 6166 ex-Works 24 November 1957.** These were the first locomotives in each class to be repainted green and fully lined out. *W. Potter*

Above: **No 3100 with No 1422, 29 September 1957.** *Hugh Ballantyne*

Above right: **Lt-rt No L90 (London Transport), 4565, 5538, 4563, 5 November 1961.** *Hugh Ballantyne*

Right: **No 1013** *County of Dorset* **ex-Works, 25 October 1955.** *Rev A. Newman*

2-2-2s Nos 69-76 worked three turns to Neath and back daily, Ahrons saying that for their size, they were about the best single driver express engines and were remarkably fast runners. In the same period, Swindon also had 6ft 6in coupled '2201' class 2-4-0 engines Nos 2205-10 which worked two turns to Weymouth, one to Neath and one on Saturdays to Taunton. The Neath trip was a marathon. The crew booked on at 6.50am, the train leaving at 7.50 for the 262-mile return run. There were 32 intermediate stops in each direction and a two hour wait at Neath. Swindon was reached at 8.05pm, the exhausted crew booking off about 9.00pm. In 1887 the Swindon links were rearranged and Nos 2201-10 had one London

turn; three Neath turns and one Cardiff run via Gloucester; one Neath turn via the Severn Tunnel, two Weymouth trips and a Saturday trip to Taunton. The London turn came back on the 5.10pm express. Leaving Paddington with 16 six-wheeled coaches, five coaches for Windsor were slipped at Slough; three more for Taplow; a further three dropped off at Twyford for Henley, drawing up at Reading with only five of the original 16 coaches.

George Jackson Churchward, then Assistant Loco Superintendent was appointed Swindon's first mayor in 1900 when the Old Town and New Town became one municipality. Appointed CME in 1902, using the best of British, American and

French practice, he introduced highly efficient locomotives using a system of standard components, combinations of which could be worked into a wide range of different locomotives. He produced the 'Star' 4-6-0s, the ancestor of many classes of locomotive, not all of them Great Western. Another important innovation was the first stationary locomotive testing plant in the country which he set up in 1904. Modernised in the mid-1930s to absorb more power it proved invaluable in the 1950s improving performance of 'Kings' and 'Castles'. Churchward retired in December 1921 but kept in close contact with the Works, and while crossing the main line on 19 December 1933 on one of his almost daily visits, he was instantly killed by No 4085 *Berkeley Castle* hauling the 8.55am Paddington-Fishguard express.

One of the unusual classes seen at Swindon was de Glehn Atlantics, c1905 No 102 *La France* with 12 corridors, 330 tons behind the tender, covering the 118.5 miles from Bristol to Paddington in 118 minutes. Another interesting engine was the unique Great Western Pacific No 111 *The Great Bear* whose weight limited

it to the London to Bristol line on which it worked both express passenger trains and fast fitted freights, the latter also being worked by mixed traffic 2-8-0s of the '47xx' class handling up to 70 vehicles. Rather surprisingly, tank engines too were used between London and Bristol and in 1907 it is recorded that the 5.30am newspaper and mail train from Paddington was worked to Bristol by a 4-4-2 'County' tank engine equipped with water pick up apparatus, returning on the 9.35am from Bristol running non-stop from Swindon Junction to Paddington in 87 minutes slipping a coach at Reading. No 2935 *Caynham Court* was fitted with rotary cam poppet valve gear in May 1931 and shedded at Swindon for much of the remainder of its life.

On 6 April 1959 stopping trains on the Swindon to Weston-super-Mare line were dieselised. A little later 'Warships', 'Westerns', 'Hymeks' and Class

Below: **Contrasting generations at Swindon, both foreigners: BR Standard Class 4MT No 75067 and ex-Taff Vale No 322. 11 September 1955.** *Hugh Ballantyne*

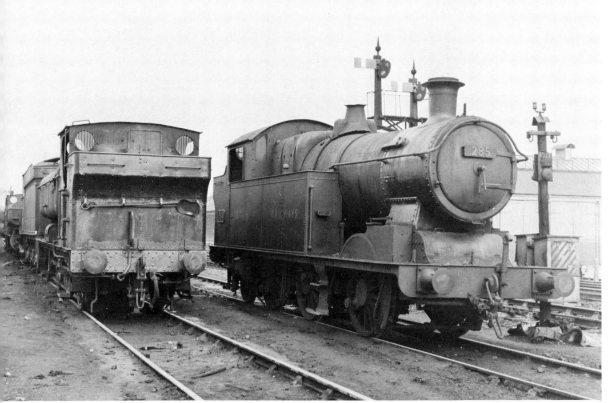

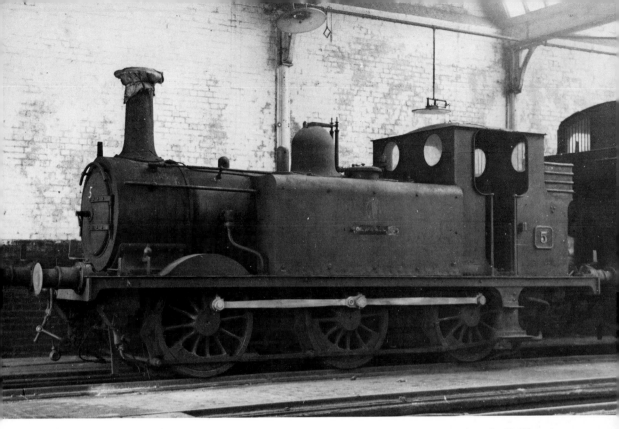

Above left: **Ex-Cardiff Railway No 682, 26 May 1954.**
Hugh Ballantyne

Left: **No 285 ex-Taff Vale right and No 7710 left, on reception roads, 23 February 1958.** *Hugh Ballantyne*

Above: **GWR No 5 inside Swindon Stock Shed 1952. This locomotive had come from the Weston, Clevedon & Portishead Light Railway which had bought it from the London, Brighton & South Coast Railway.** *W. Potter*

47s appeared on expresses and in 1968-9 the line from Paddington to Bristol was the hunting ground of No D0280 *Falcon* which, in the author's experience, was an excellent engine always to be relied upon to arrive punctually. Class 50s made redundant by London Midland Region West Coast electrification superseded Class 47s and 'Westerns' on Paddington-Bristol trains on 6 May 1974, though many failures occurred initially because on Brunel's main line, the locomotives were having to run at their full speed longer than they had been required to do before. Following trial runs between London and Bristol on 16-19 December 1974, IC125 No 252.001 appeared on some trains in 1975, a regular service beginning in the spring of 1977.

In the 1920s and 1930s the Sheffield train was worked in some months by LNER engines and some by GWR. LNER 'C1' class Atlantics working the service included Nos 3276/7, 3295, 4428, 4433/4, 4449, 4-4-0 'Directors' Nos 5437 *Prince George*, 5501 *Mons* and 5502 *Zeebrugge*. In 1937 'Sandringhams' took over the turn, Nos 2863 *Everton*, 2864 *Liverpool* and 2865 *Leicester City* being regulars. After World War 2 the train was worked by 'B1' class 4-6-0s.

The first recorded locomotive on the Highworth branch was 4-4-0ST No 13 which worked on the branch 1897-1901. In 1902 '517' class 0-4-2Ts and '850' class 0-6-0STs are recorded as working. After the disappearance of the '850' class, latterly both pannier and saddle tank varieties, it was decreed that only four-coupled engines should run over the branch, six-coupled engines requiring special authority. 'Metro' 2-4-0Ts occasionally put in an appearance. In 1926 GWR No 12, an 0-4-0 geared locomotive with vertical engine and boiler built by the Sentinel Waggon Co Ltd No 6515 was tried on the Highworth and a few other branches, but found unsuitable, was taken out of service and returned to the makers in January 1927. Workmen's trains were hauled by the Carriage Finishing Shop shunter. Collett 0-4-2Ts of the '48xx' and '58xx' classes worked

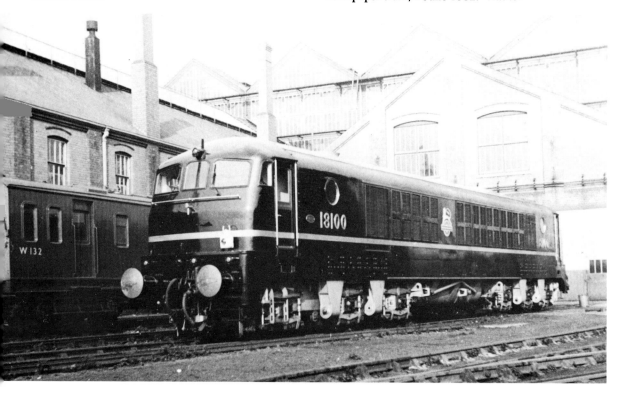

Below: Gas turbine No 18100 at Swindon c1952.
M. E. J. Deane

Bottom: No 31.131 at Swindon with up empty
newspaper train, 2 June 1982.   *Author*

the branch latterly, '1366' class 0-6-0PTs with outside cylinders very occasionally appearing and the '16xx' 0-6-0PTs. By 1960 the '03' class diesel 0-6-0 shunters appeared on freight and latterly on workmen's trains.

One of the features of Swindon Works were the 0-6-4 crane tank engines. Their fronts were similar to that of the '850' class, but domes omitted to accommodate the jibs in the travelling position. No 16 *Hercules* was built in April 1921 and Nos 17 *Cyclops* and No 18 *Steropes* in April 1901. Nos 16 and 18 worked at Swindon and No 17 at Stafford Road Works, Wolverhampton until March 1934 when it was transferred to Swindon. All these engines were withdrawn in September 1936, although more than a year elapsed before they were broken up. Another crane tank used at Swindon was No 1299, originally *Jupiter*, a standard gauge 2-4-0 side tank built for the South Devon Railway in 1878. Fitted with a crane in April 1881, for many years before its withdrawal in September 1936 it was a familiar sight outside the Works. One frequent scene at Swindon was a goods train with a small engine, not in steam, coupled behind the train engine. The outside rods were removed for the trip to the Works and placed in the bunker.

The original GWR engine shed at Swindon officially opened 1 January 1843, but records show that it was partially in use for some months prior to that date. Situated near the junction of the Gloucester branch beside Milepost 77¾, it was constructed of timber with stone corners and slated roof. The dimensions of the running shed ('A' shed) were 490ft by 72ft and it was capable of holding on four roads, 48 engines and tenders. In the centre and at right angles to the shed and abutting against its northern side, was the Engine House ('B' shed) 290ft by 140ft; divided by two rows of columns into three compartments. Locomotives stood in the side compartments, the centre being occupied by a traverser. The building, holding 36 locomotives, was used for light repairs carried out by footplate crews. The roof of

Below: 'B1' class 4-6-0 No 61369 awaiting repair at the Works, 22 January 1956. *W. Potter*

Right: Crane locomotive No 18 *Steropes* beside the original broad gauge loco shed, 11 September 1927. *H. C. Casserley*

Below right: No 3024 *Storm King* outside the original broad gauge loco shed. Notice carving of a 'Fire Fly' class engine. *LPC*

Left: **The former Chief Mechanical Engineer's offices, 2 June 1982. The carvings of a 'Fire Fly' class engine came from the original engine shed opened 1 January 1843.** *Author*

Right: **The Engine House, c1850.** J. C. Bourne

Below: **Swindon shed c1890. Note snow plough on the right.** *GWR*

Below right: **GWR brick fired at Swindon.** *Author*

Above: **Loco shed (lt-rt): No 1014** *County of Glamorgan;* **No 6864** *Dymock Grange;* **No 4950** *Patshull Hall;* **No 1013** *County of Dorset,* **1 December 1963.**
Hugh Ballantyne

Below: **Swindon Loco Yard No 1013** *County of Dorset* **1 December 1963.** *Hugh Ballantyne*

Above right: **Diesel-hydraulic Nos 813 and 825 at Swindon.** *N. Preedy*

Right: **No 6011** *King James I* **at Swindon shed 12 May 1959.** *G. Wheeler*

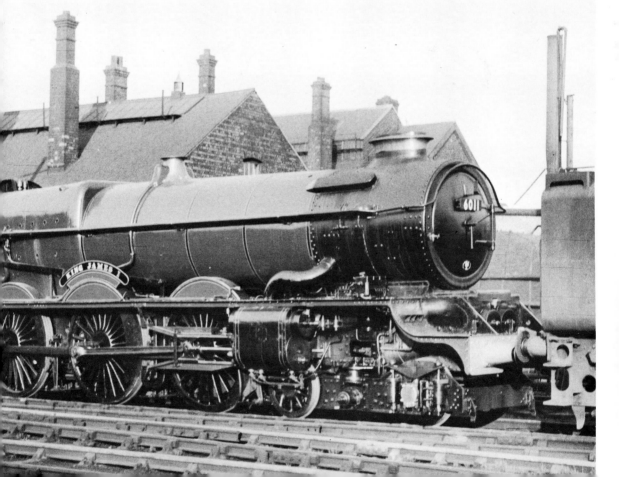

timber and wrought iron was covered with slates. Circa 1871 only the outer two roads were used for stabling broad gauge engines, the inner bay being for those awaiting entry to the Works. By 1887 all four roads were mixed and following the abolition of the broad gauge in May 1892, the shed became part of the Works. It was demolished in 1929. Both a 30ft and 40ft diameter turntable were provided. The carvings of a 'Fire Fly' class engine above the main doorway to the Chief Works manager's office came from this original shed.

In 1871 a nine road standard gauge shed was built on the up side of the Gloucester branch ready for the standard gauge rails which arrived in February 1872. 360ft by 165ft it had walls of GWR bricks and a slate roof, with a raised smoke vent to every three bays. At a later period, a turntable was installed at the north end with 21 radiating roads and three entrance/exit roads. In 1908 a roundhouse 216ft by 182ft was added to the east with 27 radiating roads. The shed had the GWR code SDN and the BR code 82C. It closed on 2 November 1964. A six road stock shed was sited further to the north and used for stabling engines not immediately required for traffic. During the Depression in the early 1930s, engines filled the shed and the outside sidings.

In 1964 train crews consisted of 174 drivers, 112 firemen 20 cleaners and over a hundred guards; in 1968 the figures were 88 drivers, 63 second men and 62 guards, while in June 1982 the respective figures were 64, 16 and 38. With faster services there is less need for crew changing at intermediate stations and today, Swindon men are mainly on freight work and the DMU service to Gloucester. Two '08' shunters work in

Above: **Swindon Loco shed, 1 December 1963 (lt-rt):** **No 1028** *County of Warwick*; **No 5904** *Kelham Hall*; **No 5002** *Ludlow Castle*, **No 4079** *Pendennis Castle.* *Hugh Ballantyne*

Right: **Roundhouse, Swindon 30 August 1953 (lt-rt):** **No 4951** *Pendeford Hall*, **No 6985** *Parwick Hall* and **Standard Class 4MT No 75038.** *A. R. Carpenter*

Below: **Locomotive shed 1947.**

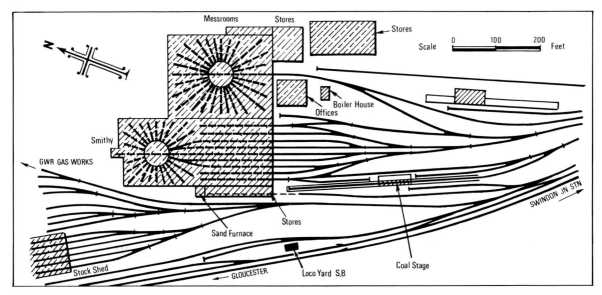

the yards east of the station: one on two shifts and one on one shift. There is no loco depot at Swindon now, just a one-road shed north-west of the station providing a fuelling point and emergency repair facility, there is normally no need for locomotives to be changed.

At its opening, the Swindon, Marlborough & Andover Railway had three small Dübs 0-6-0Ts. At first only fitted with a handbrake, Gresham & Craven's vacuum brake was added later. After the company acquired passenger engines, these locomotives were used principally on goods trains and on the twice daily trips between Swindon Town and the transfer sidings east of Swindon Junction. In September 1881 Robert Fairlie offered an 0-4-4T to the company, the driving wheels being set on a bogie allowing curves to be negotiated more easily through reduced friction. The steampipe was constantly giving way and it is possible that the loco foreman at Swindon did not fully understand the Walschaert's valve gear, but for whatever reason, its coal consumption was unduly high. The engine acquired the nickname 'Jumbo' and was certainly a white elephant. It spent a few weeks in 1888 working the Swindon transfer trips, but was generally little used.

For the opening to Andover, the SMAR required something better than goods tanks and a passen-

Left: **No 2954** *Tockenham Court* **by the coaling stage, Swindon shed 30 September 1951.** *W. Potter*

Below: **No 5802 still lettered GWR, alongside the coal stage 11 September 1955.** *Hugh Ballantyne*

Right: **ROD No 3028 outside loco shed 6 May 1956.** *Hugh Ballantyne*

Below right: **Swindon Stock Shed 21 September 1952. Left 2-8-0T No 4264 and 'Star' class 4-6-0 No 4059** *Princess Patricia* **right.** *W. Potter*

ger engine which could 'never be depended on', so three standard Beyer Peacock 2-4-0Ts were bought, two being based at Swindon. One worked the two daily trips each way and the other one trip in each direction and part of the goods service. The third worked passenger and mixed trains on the Swindon to Cirencester service. The following year a similar but larger engine was purchased. With the subsequent development of the Midland & South Western Junction Railway as it had then become, various other engines were bought. In 1895 the railway acquired a Beyer peacock 2-6-0 which at the time of purchase, was

the only example of this wheel arrangement in the country. A very successful engine, 'Galloping Alice' on one occasion hauled a 62-wagon goods train from a standing start at Rushey Platt Low Level, to Swindon Town in eight minutes, a distance of 1¾ miles up a gradient of 1 in 75. MSWJR men believed that Churchward living at Newburn, Swindon, saw how well it coped with heavy goods trains and was encouraged to build one himself. After Grouping, the Great Western-ised No 24 consistently worked the Swindon to Stoke Gifford goods from 1925 to 1930. In the last 24 years of its existence, the MSWJR standardised on 4-4-0s and 0-6-0s.

At various times the MSWJR was worked by foreign engines. The LSWR lent three in 1882; two Beattie 2-4-0s were loaned in 1891, while during World War 1 MR 4-4-0s and 0-6-0s, LSWR 4-4-0s; GWR 0-6-0 tank engines, 'Dean Goods' 0-6-0s and 'Bulldog' 4-4-0s appeared. Following the Grouping 'Dukes' assisted the MSWJR 4-4-0s with the through trains, some of the engines used being No 3258 *The Lizard*, 3260 *Mount Edgcumbe*, 3261 *St Germans*, 3269 *Dartmoor*, 3284 *Isle of Jersey* and 3290 *Severn*. Each year a military tattoo lasting for a week, was held at Tidworth. Excursion trains were worked to Swindon Junc-

Left: **No 9024 in steam, outside the Locomotive Stock Shed, 29 September 1957.** *Hugh Ballantyne*

Below left: **Outside Swindon Stock Shed, September 1964, (lt-rt): Nos 4564, 5060** *Earl of Berkeley*, **'49xx' class; Nos 6379; 6804** *Brockington Grange*; **'73xxx' class; Nos 5092** *Tresco Abbey*, **1010** *County of Caernarvon*, **1012** *County of Denbigh*; **1014,** *County of Glamorgan*. *R. A. Garland*

Below: **Loco shed, Swindon 2 June 1982.** *Author*

tion where the engine was replaced by a couple of 'Dukes' which drew the train over the MSWJR to Tidworth. As insufficient 'Dukes' were available in the area, eight to 10 of the class were transferred from the former Cambrian lines for Tattoo week. A small GWR tank engine on a running in turn worked the shuttle service between Swindon Town and Swindon Junction when MSWJR engines were at the Works for heavy repairs or rebuilding. Between 1928 and 1931 2-6-2Ts Nos 5558/9/65 were shedded at Swindon and worked the Old Town Bunk.

To permit heavier locomotives to be used, from 1930 onwards bridges were strengthed and 'Blue' classified engines took over traffic, all the MSWJR engines except the 2-4-0s being scrapped by 1938. 'Bulldogs' superseded MSWJR 4-4-0s and '43xx' Moguls replaced the MSWJR 0-6-0s. 'Dukedogs' made their trials on the line and '2251' class 0-6-0s and '51xx' class 2-6-2Ts appeared. Between 1936 and 1943 'Aberdare' 2-6-0s Nos 2639/56/79 worked the daily goods between Gloucester and Swindon Town. About 1941 'Manors' appeared, No 7808 *Cookham Manor* was probably the first, and 20 years later in 1961, was certainly the last to work on the line. During World War 2 '28xx' engines worked freight trains and Moguls were frequently used in pairs. Ministry of Supply and LMS Class 8F 2-8-0s also appeared, followed by the USA type in 1943-4.

Above: **Swindon, Marlborough & Andover Railway No 7.** *Messrs Beyer, Peacock*

Above right: **MSWJR, No 13 at Swindon Town.** *GWR*

Right: **'Dukedogs' ran their trials over the MSWJR line. No 9027 on arrival sidings awaiting withdrawal, 18 August 1957.** *W. Potter*

The first 'Castle' to work on the line was No 5085 *Evesham Abbey* which carried royalty to Swindon Town in October 1941. After World War 2, Moguls, and 'Manors' worked most of the traffic. Southern Region 'N', 'U' and more rarely 'U1' class 2-6-0s worked through Swindon Town en route from Southampton to Cheltenham.

The SMAR shed at Swindon Town was constructed close to the southern end of the station. Measuring 80ft by 35ft it was of corrugated iron with a roof of the same material. A 40ft turntable adjoined. When the station was enlarged in 1905, the shed had to be demolished to make room for the new layout. Replaced by a building some 25 chains to the south, this was constructed of brick with slated roof and measured 73ft by 39ft. Like the first, it had two roads. It closed 21 January 1924 as part of a rationalisation scheme, the men and locomotives being transferred to the GWR depot.

Above: 'U1' class No 31896 at
Swindon Town 22 July 1961.
S. P. J. A. Derek

Right: Swindon Town loco shed
29 April 1965. *Author*

Passenger stations, Goods Sheds and Preservation

The Great Western directors, anxious to keep capital expenditure to a minimum as the railway had exceeded the estimated cost of construction, signed a contract with Messrs J. & C. Rigby, builders of many of the stations, the firm constructing the station at Swindon, giving it to the GWR, which leased it back for a penny a year, the GWR undertaking to stop all passenger trains at Swindon for 10 minutes, no other stop for refreshments being allowed between London and Bristol, the idea being that Rigby's would recoup the outlay from catering profits. The permanent station buildings opened at Swindon on 14 July 1842, 19 months after the line had reached it. The station, designed by Brunel, consisted of two three-storey stone buildings 170ft by 37ft, forming two island platforms, the two inside platform roads being used by Bristol trains and the outer by those to and from Gloucester. Each platform measured 184ft by 68ft, verandahs sheltering it on all four sides supported by pillars set in pairs. It was designed with island platforms to facilitate interchange, Swindon station being the only early GWR station of importance not to incorporate an overall roof. The kitchens and offices were in the basements, the whole of the ground floors being taken up with first and second class refreshment rooms, (no facilities were provided for third class passengers), the upper floors being devoted to hotel use. The two buildings were connected by a covered footbridge, used by both passengers and hotel guests until a subway was built in 1870 after which it was only used by the hotel. The coffee and sitting rooms were on the south side and the bedrooms on the north side of the Bristol line.

The walls and ceilings of the refreshment rooms were elaborately decorated in arabesque, supported by columns 'most exquisitely painted in

Below: **Swindon Junction view up c1909.** *GWR*

99

Left: **First class refreshment room, Swindon Junction c1850.**
George Measom

Below: **First class refreshment room, Swindon Junction c1900.**
R. H. Cocks

Bottom: **Swindon Junction 1880.**

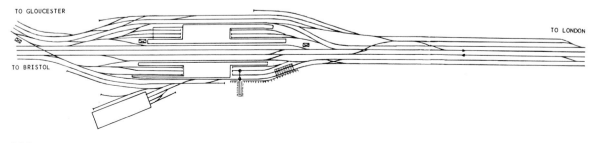

TO GLOUCESTER

TO LONDON

TO BRISTOL

imitations of inlaid woods: nor would the mirrors, hangings and furniture that adorn them, do shame in comfort and elegance to the dining-room of our first nobility'. Each refreshment room was divided into two parts by columns and an oval counter at which refreshments were sold and which separated first from second class passengers. 'A glance down yonder staircase leading to kitchens below us, amply fitted with culinary apparatus, pantries and store-rooms filled to repletion with every solid article of food that reasonable man can wish for and spacious cellars, whose bins are full of the choicest wines, and whose shelves groan under the weight of hundreds of dozens of porter, ale, soda water etc.' 'Ascend to the upper floor: there you will find a noble coffee-room, private sitting rooms, etc, (with bedrooms on the other side of the Line), in fact, all the appurtenances of a first-rate family hotel, nearly every window of which commands magnificent views of the Wiltshire and Berkshire scenery for many miles around.' — George Measom's Guide to the Great Western Railway, 1852.

Within a week of signing the lease, Rigby's agreed to let it for seven years for a premium of £6,000 and a rent of £1,100 annually to S. Y. Griffiths of the Queen's Hotel, Cheltenham. The lease ran from Christmas 1841 and the permanent building being incomplete, the subcontractor at first used temporary premises. Five weeks after opening, the GWR directors resolved that the charges and management were 'objectionable'. Although the lease gave the GWR powers to supervise the quality of the refreshments and prices, these proved difficult to enforce. In May 1845 expresses were introduced on which the Swindon stop was reduced to one minute, the GWR claiming in a law suit that 'trains to be sent express' were exempt in the lease from a 10minute stop. The Court of Chancery disagreed, believing that 'express' in this instance meant a special train, so from 26 January 1846 the stop was enforced.

In August 1848 Rigby's sold the lease outright to J. R. Phillips for £20,000. Another lawsuit took place in 1871 when the mail train in each direction stopped for only five minutes. The Postmaster General had ordered that from 1 November 1871 the 9.15am Paddington to Bristol and the 2.45pm up, should be mail trains and agreed to their stopping at Swindon for five minutes. Judgement was in favour of the GWR as running under the authority of the Postmaster General, mail trains were 'not under the control of the GWR'. In April

1875 Phillips sold the lease to G. Moss for £45,000, the new owner improved the quality of the food, the refreshment rooms becoming one of the best in the country. The lease was sold to J. W. Chater in June 1880 for £35,000, changing hands only a year later to H. G. Lake for £70,000 and the quality of the food deteriorated. From 1 October 1895 the 10 minutes stop was abolished as the GWR bought the lease for £100,000, the sum liquidated by an annual charge against revenue until 1920. On 1 October hundreds of employees from the Works watched the 10.15am Paddington to Penzance and the 10.45am Paddington to South Wales pass through Swindon non-stop. The silver-plated coffee urn made by Martin, Baskett & Martin of Cheltenham in the shape of *Victoria*, a 2-2-2 type engine and once used in the refreshment rooms, is now an exhibit in Swindon Railway Museum. At the turn of the century, the refreshment rooms, known as the Queen's Royal Hotel was renowned for its splendid catering, the Prince of Wales (later King Edward VII) sometimes hiring a special train to take his friends there to dinner. A Masonic Hall was part of the building on the down platform. Fresh produce for the hotel's functions was sent by train from London.

F. S. Williams wrote 'The GWR was not always very punctilious in the time spent at Swindon, and trains were sometimes started again after a halt of only seven or eight minutes. It happened on 7 August 1891 that a Mr Lowenfield joined the 3.00pm train at Paddington, with a first class ticket to Teignmouth. The time of arrival of the train at Swindon was 4.27, and it was booked to leave again, of course, at 4.37. Since he was not due to reach Teignmouth till 7.42, Mr Lowenfield, somewhat rashly perhaps, elected to take an early dinner during the Swindon stop. It may be that he demolished the peculiar fare, which Swindon dignified with the name of dinner, in eight minutes. If so, the Great Western was too fast for him, for the train only waited seven minutes, and when a presumably replete Mr Lowenfield stepped on to the platform it had gone.

'Mr Lowenfield, of course was furious. There was no further connection to Teignmouth for another four hours, and even on an August evening, there are perhaps few who would enjoy Swindon for that length of time. He accordingly decided to take the next train to Bristol, and ordered by telegraph a special train to be ready to convey him thence to Teignmouth'.

Mr Lowenfield's special may have been the last to run over the broad gauge. It cost £37.17s 0d

Above: **Swindon Junction after fire on up platform 26 March 1898.** *Collection: Sean Bolan*

(£37.85) and he paid the sum by cheque to the stationmaster at Bristol and next morning stopped it. 'The Great Western Railway brought an action for the recovery from Mr Lowenfield of the cost of the special train. He responded with a counter-claim for damages, on the ground that the railway had failed to carry him to Teignmouth and had broken its contract by not stopping at Swindon for the stipulated 10 minutes. The judge agreed that the passenger was entitled to damages on account of the premature start of the train from Swindon, which he assessed at 40 shillings (£2), and that he was also entitled to a refund of the first class fare between Bristol and Teignmouth and to the reimbursement of three shillings (15p) spent on telegrams to an anxious family. The judge did not agree, however, that the suffering which would have been caused to Mr Lowenfield and his family, was such that he was justified in ordering a special. The Great Western Railway were therefore granted the recovery of the cost of the special, and also the full costs of the action.'

About 2.30am on Saturday 26 March 1898,

men in the yard noticed what they thought was a chimney fire in the hotel on the up platform. Every fireplace in the building was examined and found to be in order, it was then noticed that flames were coming from the roof. Twenty female bar attendants and maid servants evacuated their quarters on the upper floor, the last person to leave the building being the man who was the solitary guest, though the previous night a large number of men had been staying there. Swindon Fire Brigade arrived at 3.50am and the GWR fire engine 10 minutes later. The fire was under control at 5.55am, but the block was gutted. Traffic on the up line was suspended as some of the walls had become dangerously weak and required demolition. Men on night shift in part of the Works nearest the station, flocked to aid the station staff and firemen. Liquor was removed to safety and drinking indulged in, officials as well as rank and file becoming tipsy.

All up trains had to pass through the station on the central line and reverse to the down platform. The fire started in the first class refreshment room. The chimney was Z-shaped and although swept a fortnight before, lent itself to lodgement of soot, but its shape was less important than the fact that a wooden beam ran through. Circumstances which led to the fire's rapid spread was the fact that a gale was blowing, the interior walls were lath and plaster, and the incredible system of running lead gas pipes down the flues. Some of the rooms destroyed contained costly furniture used by Queen Victoria when she visited Swindon. Charles Kislingbury, divisional superintendent at Bristol, received the message of the fire's outbreak just before 5.00am at his home in Montpelier, Bristol. Leaving Temple Meads by special train at 6.15am, the locomotive and one coach arrived in Swindon at 7.0am, an average speed of about 60mile/h. Trains started using the up line through Swindon station at 7pm on the Sunday. The end of the upper storey was never rebuilt east of the footbridge and following the fire, only board, not lodging was provided, except for station servants.

Originally passengers purchased tickets from a booking office in the Bath stone built office block south of the down Gloucester line and mounted stairs to the down platform. To reach the up platform they had to climb a further flight to the upper storey, cross the covered foot bridge and descended to the up platform. A new booking office opened in 1873 in an extension to the administrative block. By 1880, three terminal roads terminated by each end face of the station building giving six extra platforms and the main line platforms were extended in timber. In 1901 the platform lengths were: up main 577ft 9in;

down main 564ft 3in; up Gloucester 535ft and down Gloucester 656ft. That year the staff consisted of 6 inspectors, 13 passenger guards, 25 signalmen, 7 ticket collectors, 59 porters, shunters, lampmen and parcels staff, 44 goods guards, 12 clerical and telegraph operators; 50 fitters, greasers, gassers and examiners and 40 refreshment room employees, making a total of over 230. Additionally a large number of goods guards worked trains to Swindon and spent the night there coming from Paddington, Yeovil, Neath, Aberdare, Newport, Cardiff and Reading. 5,000 wagons passed through Swindon daily. 17 up and the same number of down passenger trains ran between Swindon and Paddington daily. Vehicles for parcels and bicycle traffic were attached and detached at the station by seven shunting horses.

Late in 1904 the down platform was extended at both ends, while an extension of the up platform was inspected by Colonel H. A. Yorke on 28 February 1911 together with a new signalbox, Swindon Station East, superseding East box and Branch Line box.

Signalling

Early semaphore signals at Swindon were by Saxby & Farmer, the operating wires being carried overhead to give a more direct route. In 1901 Swindon Junction was worked by nine signalboxes: A, B, C, D, E, F and K on the main line; G for the Gloucester branch; H commanding the down South Wales arrivals. K box was only used for exchange traffic with the MSWJR. All but K box were open 24 hours a day. Swindon West

Below: **Swindon Junction, view down 23 July 1922. Adjustable loading gauge at No 7 bay platform used by Highworth trains. Nearest coach is a six-wheel brake third.** *LGRP courtesy David & Charles*

box opened 31 December 1913 to replace the old Swindon West and Gloucester Junction boxes as well as a small box on the Goucester branch platform. The original frame held 163 levers and was subsequently extended to 174. On the front hung an iron casting of a lion's head which had previously hung on Swindon 'C' cabin in 1880.

Signalboxes in the Swindon Area 1968

Name	Number of levers
Highworth Jc	Not known
Goods Yard	42
Swindon East	79
Swindon West	172
Rodbourne Lane	30
Rushey Platt Junction	27
Rushey Platt Station	30
Swindon Town A	25
Swindon Town B	45
Loco Yard	30

From 4 March 1968 colour light signals have been worked from a power box situated on the old down platform. Controlling $87\frac{3}{4}$ route miles, it takes over from the Reading Panel just east of Challow at Milepost $63\frac{1}{4}$ and extends to Corsham (99 miles) on the Bath line; Hullavington (97 miles) on the Severn Tunnel line and to a point midway between Kemble and Sapperton on the Gloucester line. In 1982 about 176 signals were controlled from the box. Hot box detectors are provided on the down line at Bourton, just west of

Left: **Swindon Junction, view down. Small engine shed in up bay platform, train from Gloucester on right, c1895.** *GWR*

Bottom left: **Swindon Junction, down Gloucester platform c1909.** *GWR*

Below: **Swindon Junction c1910.** *Author's Collection*

Shrivenham, and at Wootton Bassett on the up road. Swindon was the first on the Western Region to have detectors to notify signalmen of a hot axle box. At $\frac{3}{4}$-mile from the junction, the Gloucester line was singled on 28 July 1968 to Kemble, a distance of $12\frac{1}{2}$ miles. The lines from Wantage Road to Wootton Bassett are signalled for reversible working, it being one of the few such lines in the country, and Wootton Bassett to Hullavington and Thingley Junction will be so signalled when funds permit. It is a useful facility to allow an express to overtake a freight, or if there is a breakdown, it enables trains to overtake a failure. Three men operate the Swindon box for each of the three shifts, plus one stand by for each shift. The latter holds a driving licence and goes out if points are not working, or a signal fails, a van for his use being parked outside the box.

By 1929 the platforms at Swindon Junction were No 1, down loop used by Gloucester trains; Nos 2 and 3, the down bay roads; No 4 the down main; No 5 the up main; Nos 6 and 7, the up bays,

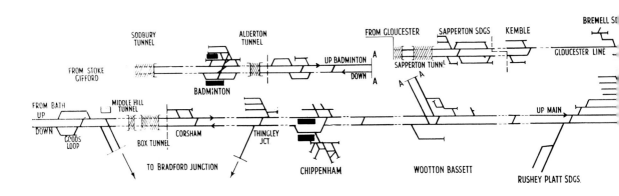

Left: **No 1155 at Swindon Junction 1933.**
Courtesy Pendon Museum

Above: **View to station from junction of Bristol and Gloucester lines c1890. White posts support overhead signal wires.** *GWR*

Below: **Swindon MAS area.**

No 6 being used by trains to the GCR and No 7 for the Highworth branch; No 8, up loop used by trains from Gloucester. At one period there was a small engine shed on Platform No 6. Movement of vehicles into the bay lines was required to be carried out with great care, no loose shunting being permitted. A special Highworth branch restricted load gauge was fixed over No 7 bay, the normal position of the sweep being at the height of 15ft above rail level, the sweep being lowered to

12ft 6in to gauge traffic for the Highworth branch. Bell pushes were provided on the up and down platforms communicating with the East and West signalboxes respectivley for the purpose of indicating to the signalmen when trains were ready to leave. Pushes were operated by the inspector or foreman in charge, but passenger shunters worked the bells for the removal of empty coaches from the platform. A train waiting to leave No 7 for Highworth blew one 'crow' on its whistle, while a train wishing to run into the bay off the down main, blew three short whistles. At Highworth Junction a train entering or leaving the up loop would blow one short and two crows. Branch trains in either direction to or from the main line blew two short whistles.

A telephone with a loud sounding bell was provided by the water column on the up through line to enable enginemen of trains which had stopped for relief purposes or water, to advise the Swindon East signalman when they were ready to

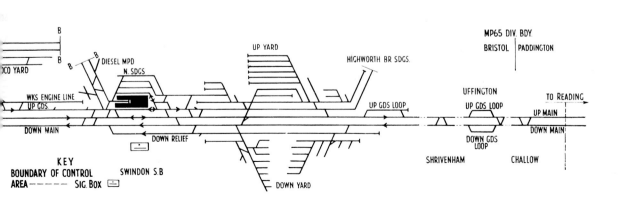

move forward. The loud sounding bell was provided to enable the signalman to attract the attention of the enginemen standing at the signals. As the signalman at Swindon West box was not always in a position to see the tail lamp on a train arriving at Platform No 8, the inspector or foreman in charge of the platform was required to telephone advising the signalman that the train was complete.

Petrol trolleys used by the Running & Maintenance Carriage Works and Stores Department at Swindon crossed the up and down engine lines and the up Gloucester main line at the Bristol end of the Gloucester line platform, after the man in charge of the trolley had obtained permission to cross from the watchman at the Wagon Works Cabin and Ground Frame. Before the watchman gave permission to the driver, he sent three beats on the bell to Swindon West signalbox indicating 'May trolley cross?' If the signalman could permit the operation he repeated the code. When the trolley cleared the crossing, the watchman sent one beat on the bell to the signalman. The watchman was required to see that no engine was approaching the level crossing on the up and down engine lines and placed the two signals for

those lines at Danger. Crossing during fog or falling snow was prohibited.

On 9 May 1921 the staff at Swindon station consisted of the following. Passenger Staff: 5 booking clerks, 2 station clerks, 2 parcels clerks, 4 platform inspectors, 24 passenger guards, 15 shunters, 24 signalmen, 3 assistant signalmen, 6 telegraphists, 10 ticket collectors, 1 train ticket collector, 2 foremen passenger and goods, 2 leading parcels porters, 24 porters, 1 travelling parcels porter, 8 parcels porters, 2 signal lampmen, 4 station lampmen, 3 lamp lads, 2 cloakroom porters and one charwoman.

Goods Staff: 7 yard inspectors, 55 goods guards, 39 shunters, 3 office porters, and 2 lad porters. It is recorded that 156,578 parcels were

Below: **Swindon Panel box 14 October 1968.** *BR*

Bottom: **Swindon Junction 1983.**

Right: **Station announcer sitting at the console on left in the Swindon Panel box, 14 October 1968.** *BR*

Below right: **Panel, Swindon MAS box 14 October 1968.** *BR*

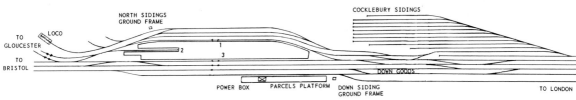

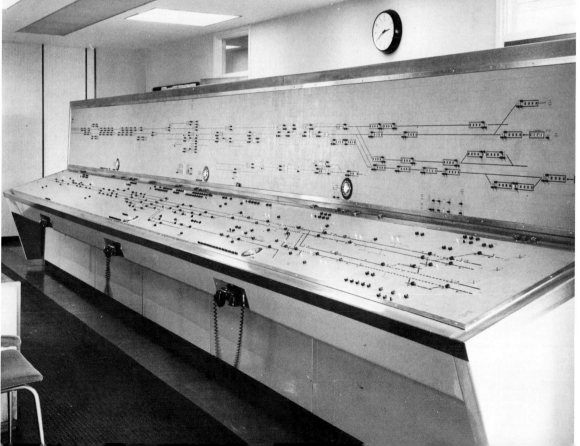

handled in 1919 and 138,926 the following year.

With the withdrawal of local trains, fewer plat-forms were required and the layout was rationalised by concentrating all traffic requiring a platform, to the former up island platform, the new layout saving passengers who are changing trains from changing platforms; it also eased staffing problems, especially ticket collectors and saved on maintenance. A 12-storey Hambro Life office block was built on the site of the old entrance block. The new layout was brought into use on 3 March 1968 coinciding with the introduction of the new signalbox. The platforms were renumbered, the station having two through roads for reversible working: the northern being No 1 and the southern No 3, with the bay platform at the west end being No 2. The capacity of the platforms is: No 1, engine and 12 coaches; No 3, engine and 13; No 2, four-car DMU. Although the through platforms are signalled for reversible working, normally No 1 is for up trains, No 3 for down, and No 2 for the Gloucester DMU. Fabric and sand are between the rails on the bay road to soak up oil from standing DMUs. The parcels plat-form was brought into use 8 May 1976, this plat-form also being used for football specials so that fans' behaviour does not upset other passengers.

Access to and from the street frontage and travel centre is by subway. A buffet and bar are on the ground floor at the west end of the building on the island platform, with toilets, bookstall and

Left: **Fabric and sand on track serving Platform No 2, to soak up oil. 2 June 1982.** *Author*

Below left: **Buffet, Swindon. 24 August 1982.** *Author*

Right: **View up, Platform 1. Note glass roof lighting platform; also concrete protection to awning support pillars. 2 June 1982.** *Author*

Below: **Swindon from south-west, 2 June 1982.** *Author*

Above: **Ticket windows, travel centre, Swindon, 24 August 1982.** *Author*

Left: **Clerk working in Swindon booking office 2 June 1982.** *Author*

Right: **Red Star parcels office 2 June 1982.** *Author*

ticket collector's booth at the east end. A Forces' Movements office is on No 3 platform, troops going to and from local camps and RAF stations by bus. Automatic doors worked by pressure on a mat give access to the platforms from buffet and vestibule. The bases of the cast iron platform canopy pillars are protected by crude concrete castings made from oil drums. Offices are on the first floor. Today although the upper storey is Bath stone, at platform level the building is cement rendered.

The travel centre opened about 1975 when three separate offices — booking, personal enquiry and telephone enquiry, were combined. Before being united, one department could be under extreme pressure and the others lightly worked, for there was no means of transferring staff, passengers had to queue for a travel ticket and a queue for a reservation — now there is just one queue. Swindon pioneered the single queue system in the West of England Division, the advantage being that a customer does not have to gamble on which queue to join to see the clerk behind the counter the quickest. The system works well. The old booking office opened 05.00 until 01.00; now it opens 06.00 till 20.00 for booking, passengers outside these hours paying the ticket collector.

The West of England Division pioneered the idea of a combined office with clerks on rotating turns on each section of work — it is more interesting for them and gives better flexibility. For example, if it is a fine day and Weston-super-Mare is popular, should telephone enquiries be light, a man can be transferred to booking. One female clerk at the Centre is on a new job — business travel survey, which involves finding out any problems firms have using railways and their requirements. As well as dealing with rail facilities, Swindon Travel Centre sells package holidays, luggage insurance, continental travel and air travel. Large firms are supplied with tickets, some printed and some blank. The active Travel Centre Manager canvasses firms and organisations in the area seeking sales. The Travel Centre has used NCR Type 51 machines since 1974, prior to that it used Edmondson card tickets. An APTIS machine, a line computer instrument, is scheduled for installation towards the end of 1983. Swindon ticket sales:

	1976	1980
	236,506	304,520
season	3,651	7,098

(In 1982 about 400 passengers daily used season tickets)

280 staff are under the Area Manager at Swindon: chief clerk, signalmen, drivers, guards, shunters etc, about 266 being at Swindon itself, 4 at Kemble and 10 at Chippenham.

It is hoped that the Red Star parcels office near the station entrance will be rebuilt in the near future. As well as parcels being carried by this service, solicitors' papers, and documents for printing firms travel by Red Star. When a package is brought in, it is weighed, paid for, labelled, card indexed and taken over to a nominated train, either carried by hand, or in a BRUTE trolley. Swindon deals with approximately 400 Red Star parcels weekly.

The goods depot situated $\frac{3}{4}$-mile east of Swindon Junction, was a large structure of brick, corrugated iron, corrugated asbestos and corrugated plastic coated metal, with three roads under cover. Latterly used by National Carriers, the building is now disused. The GWR started its own motor lorry delivery service from Swindon in 1928 and it proved to be cheaper than using local carters.

Stratton station on the Highworth branch opened 9 May 1883. It had a timber building, with a corrugated iron pagoda provided later to serve as a parcels office and waiting room. The double doors to the main building, led to the

booking office on the left and ladies' waiting room and lavatory on the right. The timber building was extended to accommodate a ground frame and when this closed on 4 June 1909, it was used as a stationmaster's office, later becoming a store. The station at one time was very busy with milk traffic and the single platform had no less than 15 platform trolleys. There was a goods loop and two sidings. The corrugated iron goods shed stood on a brick plinth beside the loop. Arkell's brewery at Kingsdown brought hops, malt, sugar and coal traffic to the station and beer was despatched in small quantities. Other traffic included cattle cake and potatoes. The station closed to passengers 2 March 1953, became a coal depot only from 19 May 1964 and closed completely on 4 October 1965.

Stratton Park Halt on the main line $2\frac{1}{4}$ miles east of Swindon Junction, opened 20 November 1933 and closed 7 December 1964, when stopping passenger services ceased between Swindon and Didcot.

The brick built MSWJR station, Swindon Town, locally known as Old Town station, at first had two platforms, but in 1904-5 was enlarged when the up platform became an island, the centre run-round road being removed at the same time. It was the second largest station on the MSWJR, the platform faces totalling 1,548ft and was situated on a sharp curve. By 1885 a footbridge, open top with high sides, connected the platforms. The outer face of the island platform was used by shuttle trains to Swindon Junction. The station closed to passenger traffic on 11 September 1961 but the refreshment rooms on the down platform remained in use until January 1965. The down platform had a well-kept garden overlooked by

Top left: **Parcels platform, 2 June 1982.** *Author*

Centre left: **Swindon's newest railway structure: County Road Bridge being built 2 June 1982, $\frac{1}{4}$-mile east of Swindon station. Up empty newspaper train from Bristol. Bridge works involved the line being completely closed from Maundy Thursday to Easter Monday in 1981 and 1982.** *Author*

Bottom left: **North side of Swindon goods shed, 2 June 1982.** *Author*

Below: **Former goods shed from south-west. 2 June 1982.** *Author*

Right: **Stratton, October 1966.**
D. J. Hyde

Below: **Swindon Town shortly after 1904-5 alterations. Notice the repeater signal on the left just in front of the footbridge.**
Author's collection

The Croft, headquarters of the MSWJR. The station had a cattle pen, horse dock, goods shed, 55ft turntable and water tower. The original engine shed near the south end of the station was replaced by a new structure further south when the island platform was put in. It was about this time that the goods shed was enlarged and rebuilt in brick. On the up side of the line were smiths' and carpenters' shops and a sheet repairing depot. The down goods loop joined the down main almost 1,000yd from the controlling box Swindon Town B. In order that when the time came for a freight to move the fireman did not have to walk nearly 2,000yd, an auxiliary token was used. The

goods yard handled general freight until 19 May 1964, closed to coal traffic 3 November 1966 and to Esso traffic late in 1968. It formed the railhead for M4 Motorway stone traffic 1970-1.

Rushey Platt, $1\frac{1}{2}$ miles west of Swindon Junction had its four platforms on two different levels; the MSWJR main line being high as it had just crossed the GWR, the two platforms on the branch to the GWR placed at a lower level. These latter two were staggered. The high level platforms were connected by subway. The station closed 1 October 1905, but as late as 1935 trains still stopped unofficially to allow the occupants of the low level station, converted to a dwelling, to alight. The high level platforms, shortened, continued to be used for milk traffic. The station closed to freight, excluding coal and private sidings, on 19 May 1964.

An interesting calamity occurred at the station on 26 June 1895. The lurching of the 3.10pm from Andover as it passed from one curve to another near the turnout, caused a light four-wheeled LSWR truck to become derailed shortly after passing through the loop points at the southern end of the station. It was dragged along the ballast beside the line for a quarter of a mile, striking the projecting ends of the platform's wooden joists and knocking them out of place so that the platform collapsed down the slope of the embankment. The stationmaster, waiting to receive the tablet, fell with the platform and was thrown down the embankment, luckily suffering only bruises. The signalman, further along the 150yd platform, ready to give the tablet for the

Left: **D7044 at Swindon Town, view south 29 April 1965.** *Author*

Above: **Swindon Town 'B' signalbox 29 April 1965.** *Author*

Right: **The 1917 built LSWR style MSWJR signalbox at Rushey Platt station with single line token apparatus beyond. 21 April 1965.** *Author*

Left: **Gangers' motor trolley outside Rushey Platt signalbox 1947.**
M. Boucher

Below: **Rushey Platt.** *D. J. Hyde*

Below: The western environs of Swindon looking back from a down train to the overbridge carrying the MSWJR at Rushey Platt Junction. On the embankment are sighting signals and ground frame to operate them. 20 September 1964. *D. J. Hyde*

Below right: **Moredon 1934.**
LGRP, courtesy David & Charles

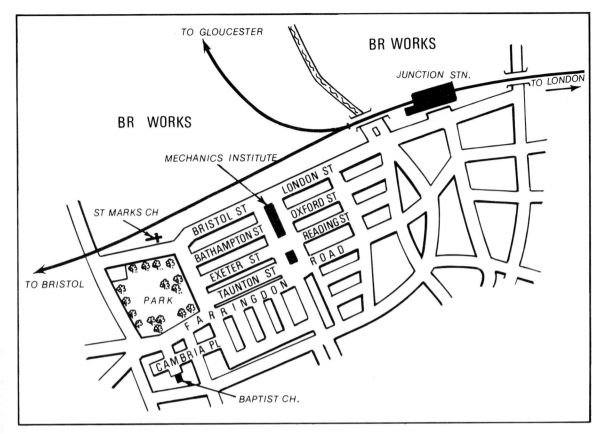

Above: **Railway village.**

section ahead, saved himself by running down the bank at the north end of the station. The accident was caused by excessive speed.

North of the station, the main GWR Paddington to Bristol line was crossed by a bridge of wrought iron plate girders resting on masonry abutments and spanning 92½ft. On the embankment close to the GWR line were three signals facing the GWR Works and used for testing locomotive men's eyesight. They were worked from an adjoining ground frame. The MSWJR passed the west end of the Dump and went under the Cheltenham & Great Western Union Railway.

The sleeper-faced, 40ft long Moredon Platform opened 25 March 1913 on the south side of the road bridge and on the west side of the line, principally dealt with milk traffic. In 1928 sidings were laid to the electricity works, 100 coal wagons being handled daily in 1950. The platform closed 1 October 1932.

The GWR directors provided housing for the workers at the new railway factory, 300 cottages being built south of the line. Designed by Sir Matthew Digby Wyatt, architect of Paddington station, the streets led off from Emlyn Square, the western ones being Bristol, Bath, Exeter and

Taunton Streets which were built first in 1845 and those to the east — London, Oxford, Reading and Faringdon Streets when the western ones were completed. Bath Street was renamed Bathampton Street c1902. Unusual for contemporary artisans' houses, they had a small garden in front giving the street a spacious air, while at the back was a yard containing a wash house and privy. Built by J. & C. Rigby & Co and at their expense, Messrs Rigby recovered the money from rents collected by the GWR. Although each house had a tap, the water was not always potable and an enterprising man was kept busy selling fresh spring water at a halfpenny a bucketful. The estate was bought by Swindon Council in 1966 and three years later began tastefully modernising the railway village, the homes being provided with bathrooms and new kitchens. Under Wyatt's plans, the occupants had only the village slipper baths where cleanliness was rationed. If the clocked time of a bath was exceeded, the attendant, from the outside, pulled out the plug. Today the fact that council houses can be sold has brought problems as the council wishes to preserve the village as an entity, whereas central government considers them ordinary council houses. The buildings in the village also include three public houses — the 'Glue Pot', 'Cricketer's Arms' and 'Baker's Arms'.

The GWR was a thoughtful, considerate employer providing far more than just housing facilities. G. H. Gibbs, a director, in 1842 left £500 in his will towards building a church and school for the railway village. Designed in Early English style by Gilbert Scott, St Mark's cost £6,000, the remainder being raised by public subscription as the company was unable to use share capital for the purpose. It was consecrated 25 April 1845. Until 1850 the GWR paid the vicar's stipend of £120 per annum. The grave and obelisk of Joseph Armstrong, the first GWR Locomotive, Carriage & Wagon Superintendent is prominent in the churchyard. In March 1960 a new peal, 'Evening Star Delight Minor' was composed and rung for the last locomotive to be built in the town.

The Mechanics' Institute was built in Tudor style, architect Edward Roberts, to provide facilities for mutual improvement classes; library, (no municipal library being set up in Swindon until 1943, schoolchildren proceeding in a crocodile to the GWR Library once a week, the railway library closed in 1961) and theatre. To keep abreast of social changes, in 1959 the Institute became the BR Staff Association. In 1845 the GWR opened a school, (now the BR fire station and Research Laboratory) in Bristol Street, at first for children of its employees, but later admitting others. Fees were 4d a week for juniors and 2d for infants, children of non-GWR parents having to pay a shilling (5p). In 1874 the GWR built a larger school in College Street and in 1881 handed its 1,600 pupils to the care of the local authority school board. The GWR Medical Fund provided doctors' surgeries and a dispensary. By 1948 the GWR Medical Fund Society Hospital could deal with the population of 40,000. The GWR even had its own hearse, known locally as a 'Shillibier'. The GWR supplied coal and timber to its employees at advantageous prices. Coal was delivered by horse and cart, later by motor lorry, but timber was collected from the GWR Wood Wharf in Whitehouse Road. Two grades were supplied: refuse (bark etc) and old timber, the latter being more expensive. The entrance to the wood wharf was at ground level and timber tipped down a chute from rail level about 20ft above. In order to collect the purchase ticket the attendant lowered a tin can on a piece of string or chain, the purchaser placed the ticket in the tin and it was pulled up to check if it was for 'old timber' or 'refuse'. In hard times, very often 'refuse' was ordered, but with a penny or two dropped in the tin along with the 'refuse' ticket which very often resulted in good quality 'old timber' being supplied. The GWR also provided a park (given to the Corporation in 1925), swimming and Turkish baths. Just inside the Tunnel entrance to the Works were three windows for purchasing tickets

Below left: **Railway village, Swindon 4 November 1971.** *T. G. Flinders*

Right: **The 'Glue Pot'; Emlyn Square, one of the public houses in the railway village, 16 August 1982.** *Author*

Below: **GWR Mechanics' Institute 16 August 1982.** *Author*

at one third of the public price. GWR employees had their own savings bank at Swindon which gave slightly higher interest than the main banks.

In the 1850s, accommodation in the railway village was very short, in some instances 10-12 people being in two rooms and when the night shift men rose, the day men went to bed. In 1851 over 55% of the New Swindon workers originated from outside the county. The company attempted to overcome the problem by building a large three-storeyed building to accommodate over 100 single men. Each occupant had a single room, the entrance and kitchen being common. The 'Barracks' as it was called, proved a failure as young men preferred to lodge in the village where there were fewer restrictions. The Barracks was then converted into flats, each family being allotted three rooms, with common washing facilities in the quadrangle. The community was not a happy one and the families quarrelled. In 1869 the building was converted into a Wesleyan Church. Joseph Armstrong was a local preacher and conducted services there. It was converted into a railway museum in 1962. The principal large exhibits are: 2-2-2 *North Star*, 4-4-0 No 3717 *City of Truro*, 4-6-0 No 4003 *Lode Star*, 0-6-0 No 2516 and 0-6-0PT No 9400. The driving wheels of *Lord of the Isles* are on display. In 1906 the GWR offered the complete engine to Swindon Education Committee for £200 provided it was fixed on a plinth in front of the Swindon & North Wilts Secondary School, but unfortunately the offer was declined, though until World War 2 the complete reversing gear, valve gear and motion was preserved on the wall of a drawing classroom. Next door to the museum is the

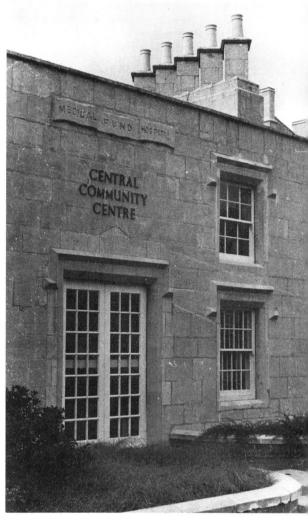
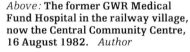

Above: **The former GWR Medical Fund Hospital in the railway village, now the Central Community Centre, 16 August 1982.** *Author*

Left: **The former GWR school, now a BR research laboratory, 16 August 1982.** *Author*

Above right: **No 4003** *Lode Star* **being taken into the Railway Museum, Swindon.** *BR*

Right: **Swindon Railway Museum: Nos 9400, 2516, 3717** *City of Truro*, **28 April 1963.** *Hugh Ballantyne*

Above: **Ex-GWR No 5637 awaiting restoration at the Swindon & Cricklade Railway depot, Blunsdon, 16 August 1982.** *Author*

Left and below left: **Swindon and Thamesdown Coats of Arms. The Borough of Thamesdown was created in 1974 under the reorganisation of local government, Swindon being its industrial and commercial centre.**

Railway Village Museum — a railwayman's cottage as it was in 1900 with gaslight etc.

The Swindon & Cricklade Railway Society have a centre at Blunsdon and hope to relay track along the former MSWJR formation to Cricklade. On 13 November 1978 it was incorporated by the Registrar of Companies at Cardiff. It is a private company and can issue shares only to a maximum of 50 shareholders. Steam locomotives being restored are 0-6-2T No 5637 which belongs to the society and No 7903 *Foremarke Hall*, privately owned. Diesel locomotives are the 0-4-0 diesel-mechanical which worked at W. D. & H. O. Wills, Swindon and the two from Pressed Steel Fisher, one of the latter will be cannibalised. There is a Thomas Smith & Son steam crane with a 20-ton main lift and 8-ton auxiliary. Built in 1940 it came from the Army, Shoeburyness.

Locomotive Allocations

Swindon GWR in steam two weeks ending 27 July 1850

2-2-2 'Fire Fly' class
Actaeon, Mazeppa, Milo, Orion, Pollux, Priam

2-2-2 'Star' class
Bright Star

2-2-2 'Prince' class
Peri, Sylph

Total 9

Swindon GWR allocation 11 January 1902

4-4-0T
13

4-6-0
36

0-4-2T '517' class
554

0-6-0 Standard Goods
607, 611, 612, 680, 783, 786, 787

0-6-0ST '850' class
858, 864, 871, 995, 1908, 1929, 1981, 2011

0-6-0ST '1076' class
950, 1281, 1289, 1294, 1567, 1617

0-6-0ST '1016' class
1067

2-2-2 'Queen' class
1123 *Salisbury*

0-6-0T ex Severn & Wye & Severn Bridge Railway
1353, 1354, 1357 *Maid Marian*

0-6-0ST ex-Cornwall Minerals Railway
1393 *Lord Robartes*, 1395, 1396, 1400

0-6-0ST '1661' class
1695

0-6-0ST '1854' class
1757

0-6-0 Dean Goods
2302, 2320, 2327, 2353, 2359, 2441, 2449, 2457, 2464, 2472, 2486, 2490, 2513, 2563

'Kruger' class
2601 (4-6-0) 2602 (2-6-0)

2-6-0 'Aberdare' class
2623, 2625, 2627, 2629, 2631, 2637, 2639, 2643, 2645, 2647, 2651

0-6-0ST '2721' class
2722, 2723, 2769, 2770, 2780, 2781

4-2-2 'Achilles' class
3013 *Great Britain*, 3074 *Princess Helena*

2-4-0 'Barnum' class
3211

2-4-0 '3232' class
3234, 3251

4-4-0 'Duke' class
3257 *Guinevere*, 3266 *St Ives*, 3313 *Cotswold*, 3320 *Meteor*

4-4-0 'Bulldog' class
3339 *Marco Polo*, 3358 *Godolphin*, 3366 *Restormel*, 3369 *Trelawny*

4-4-0 'Atbara' class
3375 *Edgcumbe*, 3390 *Terrible*

2-4-0 'Stella' class
3511

Total 84

Swindon GWR allocation 24 January 1914

0-6-0 Standard Goods
434, 882, 1169, 1190

0-4-2T '517' class
549, 1154, 1476

0-6-0ST '850' class
853, 858, 859, 860, 988, 994, 996, 1983

0-6-0ST ex-Cornwall Minerals Railway
1394 *Fowey*, 1398

0-6-0ST '1076' class
1613, 1619, 1660

0-6-0ST '1661' class
1672, 1678

0-6-0T '1813' class
1851

0-6-0ST '2021' class
2069

0-6-0 Dean Goods
2315, 2348, 2355, 2386, 2399, 2408, 2426, 2430, 2434, 2438, 2457, 2480, 2511, 2522

2-6-0 'Aberdare' class
2645, 2665, 2672, 2676, 2679

0-6-0ST '2721' class
2760, 2769

2-8-0 '28xx' class
2806, 2812, 2818

4-6-0 'Saint' class
2904 *Lady Godiva*, 2915 *Saint Bartholomew*, 2980 *Coeur de Lion*, 2998 *Ernest Cunard*

2-4-0 'Barnum' class
3211

4-4-0 'Bulldog' class
3323 *Etona*, 3337 *The Wolf*, 3413, 3438, 3440, 3441 *Blackbird*, 3442 *Bullfinch*

2-4-0 'Stella' class
3511

4-4-0 '3521' class
3543, 3546

0-4-2T '3571' class
3576

4-4-0 'County' class
3821 *County of Bedford*

2-6-0 '43xx' class
4337

Total 66

Swindon GWR allocation 15 June 1947

0-6-0PT '850' class
992, 2014, 2017

0-6-0PT '1366' class
1366, 1369, 1371

0-4-2T Collett
1400, 1433, 1436, 1446, 1453, 5800, 5802, 5804, 5805

0-6-0PT '1501' class
1542

0-6-0PT '1854' class
1731, 1758

0-6-0PT '2021' class
2060

0-6-0ST ex-Burry Port & Gwendraeth Valley Railway
2195

0-6-0 '2251' class
2224, 2250

0-6-0 Dean Goods
2568

4-6-0 'Saint' class
2908 *Lady of Quality*, 2913 *Saint Andrew*, 2927 *Saint Patrick*, 2934 *Butleigh Court*, 2935 *Caynham Court*, 2945 *Hillingdon Court*, 2947 *Madresfield Court*, 2949 *Stanford Court*, 2954 *Tockenham Court*

4-4-0 'Bulldog' class
3421, 3452 *Penguin*

2-4-0T 'Metro'
3561

0-6-0PT '8750' class
3645, 3666, 3682, 3684, 3724, 3737, 3739, 3748, 3780, 4651, 4697, 8779, 9600, 9720, 9721, 9772, 9773, 9790, 9795

4-6-0 'Star' class
4015 *Knight of St John*, 4017 *Knight of Liége*, 4022, 4036 *Queen Elizabeth*, 4055 *Princess Sophia*, 4057 *Princess Elizabeth*, 4062 *Malmesbury Abbey*

2-6-0 '43xx' class
4381, 5322, 5367, 5371, 5396, 6320, 6322, 6340, 6357, 6358, 6360, 6374, 6384, 6387, 7321

2-6-2T '45xx' class
4502, 4507, 4510, 4521, 4538, 4543, 4544, 4550, 4551, 4585, 4590, 4592, 5510, 5534, 5563, 5566

4-6-0 'Hall' class
4905 *Barton Hall*, 4925 *Eynsham Hall*, 4945 *Milligan Hall*, 4956 *Plowden Hall*, 5934 *Kneller Hall*, 5943 *Elmdon Hall*, 5978 *Bodinnick Hall*, 6902 *Butlers Hall*, 6935 *Browsholme Hall*, 6965 *Thirlestaine Hall*

4-6-0 'Castle' class
5067 *St Fagans Castle*, 5068 *Beverstone Castle*

0-6-0PT '57xx' class
6716, 6737, 6739, 6741, 7792, 7794, 8733

0-6-0PT '74xx' class
7415, 7418, 7424

4-4-0 'Earl' class
9011, 9018, 9023

0-6-0PT '94xx' class
9400

Total 117

Swindon allocation 27 February 1954

0-6-0PT '1366' class
1366, 1369, 1371

0-4-2T Collett
1400, 1433, 1436, 1446, 5800, 5802, 5804, 5805

0-6-0PT '16xx' class
1647, 1648

0-6-0PT '2021' class
2060

0-6-0 '2251' class
2224

2-8-0 '28xx' class
2818, 2852, 2865, 2868

4-6-0 'Star' class
4062 *Malmesbury Abbey*

2-8-0T '42xx' class
4254, 5226, 5240

2-6-2T '45xx' class
4538, 4550, 4573, 5509, 5510, 5536, 5540, 5564, 5566

4-6-0 'Hall' class
4912 *Berrington Hall*, 4925 *Eynsham Hall*, 4972 *Saint Brides Hall*, 4973 *Sweeney Hall*, 5922 *Caxton Hall*, 5975 *Winslow Hall*, 5994 *Roydon Hall*, 5997 *Sparkford Hall*, 6915 *Mursley Hall*, 6967 *Willesley Hall*, 7914 *Lleweni Hall*, 7923 *Speke Hall*.

4-6-0 'Castle' class
5009 *Shrewsbury Castle*, 5062 *Earl of Shaftesbury*, 5068 *Beverston Castle*, 5083 *Bath Abbey*, 5084 *Reading Abbey*, 7015 *Carn Brea Castle*, 7037 *Swindon*

2-6-0 '43xx' class
5396, 6314, 6320, 6348, 6357, 6360, 6368, 6384, 6387, 7321

0-6-0PT '57xx' class
6716, 6737, 6739, 6741, 7792, 7794

4-6-0 'Grange' class
6805 *Broughton Grange*, 6832 *Brockton Grange*, 6850 *Cleeve Grange*

0-6-0PT '74xx' class
7415, 7418, 7424

0-6-0PT '94xx' class
8461, 8472, 9400, 9476

0-6-0PT '8750' class
3645, 3666, 3682, 3684, 3724, 3737, 3739, 3746, 3780, 4612, 4651, 4697, 8779, 8783, 8793, 9600, 9720, 9721, 9772, 9773, 9790, 9795

4-4-0 'Earl' class
9011, 9023

4-6-0 BR Standard Class 4MT
75000-4

2-6-0 BR Standard Class 2MT
78004

Total 107

Swindon allocation January 1965

4-6-0 'County' class
1006 *County of Cornwall*, 1010 *County of Caernarvon*, 1012 *County of Denbigh*

0-6-0PT '16xx' class
1658, 1664

0-6-0 '2251' class
2244, 2291

2-8-0 '28xx' class
2879, 2890, 3842

0-6-0PT '8750' class
3758, 4697, 6769, 9605, 9672, 9680, 9773, 9790

4-6-0 'Hall' class
4924 *Eydon Hall*, 4930 *Hagley Hall*, 5939 *Tangley Hall*, 5943 *Elmdon Hall*, 5978 *Bodinnick Hall*, 6900 *Abney Hall*, 6940 *Didlington Hall*

2-6-2T '45xx' class
5564, 5569

0-6-0PT '94xx' class
8433

4-6-0 BR Standard Class 5MT
73001, 73012, 73027

Class 03 0-6-0
D2086-8, D2126, D2143, D2144, D2146, D2182, D2186-9, D2192-4, D2196

Class 08 0-6-0
D3512, D3804, D4027, D4119, D4120-4, D4168

AC Cars 4-wheel railbus
W79975-8

Total 61

Swindon MSWJR 1923

0-6-0T
13

0-4-4T
15

0-6-0
20, 23, 27

Total 5

Bibliography

Ahrons, E. L.; *Locomotive & Train Working in the latter part of the Nineteenth Century*: Vol 4; Heffer, 1952

Allen, C. J.; *Titled Trains of the Western*; Ian Allan Ltd, 1974

Batholomew, D.; *Midland & South Western Junction Railway*. Vol 1; Wild Swan, 1982

Bradshaw's Railway Guides, (various dates)

BREL; Swindon Works, 1975

Clinker, C. R.; *Closed Stations & Goods Depots*; Avon-Anglia, 1978

Cooke, R. A.; *Track Layout Diagrams of the GWR and BR WR*, Sections 20 & 22; Author, 1974

Eversley, D. E. C.; *The Great Western Railway & the Swindon Works in the Great Depression*; University of Birmingham Historical Journal V, 1955

Grinsell, L. V.; Wells, H. B.; Tallamy, H. S.; Betjeman, J.; *Studies in the History of Swindon;* Swindon Borough Council, 1950

Hateley, R.; *Industrial Locomotives of Central Southern England*; Industrial Railway Society, 1981

Hudson, K.; *An Awkward Size for a Town*; David & Charles, 1967

Hudson, K.; 'The Early Years of the Railway Community in Swindon'; *Transport History*, Vol 1 No 2; 1968

Kelley, P.; 'This is Swindon'; *Rail Enthusiast*, June 1982

Lyons, E.; *An Historical Survey of Great Western Engine Sheds 1947*; Oxford Publishing Co, 1972

Lyons, E. & Mountford, E.; *An Historical Survey of Great Western Engine Sheds 1837-1947*; Oxford Publishing Co, 1979

MacDermot, E. T.; Clinker, C. R.; Nock, O. S.; *History of the Great Western Railway*; Ian Allan Ltd, 1964/1967

Maggs, C. G.; *The Midland & South Western Junction Railway*; David & Charles, 1980

Maggs, C. G.; *Railways of the Cotswolds*; Peter Nicholson, 1982

Marshall, J.; *A Biographical Dictionary of Railway Engineers*; David & Charles, 1978

Measom, G.; *The Official Illustrated Guide to the Great Western*; Griffin, Bohn & Co, 1852

Mountford, E. R.; *Swindon GWR Reminiscences*; Bradford Barton, 1982

Railway Correspondence & Travel Society; *Locomotives of the Great Western Railway*; RCTS, 1952-74

Silto, J; *A Swindon History 1840-1901*; Swindon, 1981

Smith, T. M.; Heathcliffe, G. S.; *The Highworth Branch*; Wild Swan, 1979

Summers, L. A.; 'Metamorphosis at Swindon Works'; *Railway Magazine*, July 1973

Vaughan, A.; *A Pictorial Record of Great Western Architecture*; Oxford Publishing Co, 1977

Victoria County History of Wiltshire, Vols 4 & 9; Oxford University Press, 1959 & 1970

Williams, A; *Life in a Railway Factory*; Duckworth, 1915

Wittamore, D.; *Signalling Record Society Newsletter*, July 1971, Sept 1971, January 1972